When God Asks for an Undivided Heart

Choosing Celibacy in Love and Freedom

Fr. Andrew Apostoli, CFR

2007

Imprimatur
+   Bernard Cardinal Law
          August 9, 1995

Published by Basilica Press
111 Fergus Court, Ste. 102
Irving, TX 75062
800-933-9398

Formerly published by Pauline Books & Media, Boston, MA
02130

Cover design: StarWorks Marketing & Communications, Stevens
Point, WI, USA
Printed in the United States of America
ISBN 978-1-9303141-0-8

Basilica Press is part of the Joseph and Marie Daou Foundation

Dedication

This book is
lovingly and gratefully dedicated
to the Blessed Virgin Mary:
the Virgin-Daughter of the Eternal Father,
the Virgin-Mother of the Son of God,
the Virgin-Spouse of the Holy Spirit.

Table of Contents

Foreword

This book is written for those whom Cardinal Newman refers to as the "resolute, undaunted, zealous few." These are "those who pass on the flame of truth in a dark world," those who are not afraid to stand before the noisy self-centered world and point out a different road.

It is no secret that, even within the Church, there are many who question vowed religious celibacy. They may question its spiritual significance or its practicality or the value of its observance. They question its real meaning in regard to clergy or to vowed laity or, incredibly, even in the lives of members of religious communities. Having uncritically accepted all the catch phrases and trends of pop psychology, the critics of celibacy often follow the path of least resistance themselves and teach others to do so.

This book by my confrere, Fr. Andrew Apostoli, a highly respected and much beloved spiritual director, restates, in clear and uncompromising ways, the traditional teachings of the Church on the much maligned practice of celibate chastity. But this book is much more than a mere statement. Just as a successful life of celibate chastity must be integrated and well balanced, the author demonstrates his own integration of this challenging tradition in his own words and life. This work is filled with a fervent and devoted love of God and with a consistent and loving concern for one's fellow human beings. Just as a vowed Christian life of celibate chastity is incomprehensible to someone who does not have a personal relationship with Christ, so the message of this book will remain obscure and perhaps even contemptible to someone whose religious practice is fundamentally external with no real response from within.

The concept of an undivided heart as the best road to a happy and productive celibate life is one that needs to be reaffirmed, as Fr. Andrew has done. My own experience suggests that, throughout the English-speaking world, there are many struggling and sincere celibates who need to hear again the classical teaching of the spiritual masters. There are also many young people who, despite poor religious education, feel called to celibate chastity as clergy, religious or vowed laity. The very existence of such an identifiable segment of a population inundated with contradictory messages on every side, indicates that the tradition of vowed religious celibate chastity is going to survive. Anyone with a sense of Church history (or even of psychological anthropology) knows that the survival of the tradition of celibate chastity is predictable. But it is still exciting to meet, everywhere one goes, "the resolute, undaunted few" who struggle against the muddy tide of popular confusion and hedonism.

It is very important in the present conflicted scene to factor out the real arguments for the tradition of vowed celibacy, to state them clearly, and to assess what a person can do to lead such a life. In my book, *The Courage to be Chaste* (Paulist Press, 1985), I discussed the practical means of living a chaste single Christian life for the vowed and the unvowed. I suggested various means for doing this, ranging from purely spiritual ones like intimacy with Christ in the sacraments, all the way to having a balanced lifestyle. Fr. Andrew addresses his book to the narrower audience of those who are already consecrated by vow or priestly oath to celibate chastity or those considering the possibility of such a commitment. Neither he nor I take up related issues like the universality of the requirement that priests be pledged to celibacy in the Western Church. That is a special issue quite distinct from the issue of vowed religious celibacy. I, in fact, have assisted several former ministers who are married men to prepare for ordination to the Catholic priesthood under the pastoral privilege. The struggles of these devout convert couples highlighted for me a number of things, including the powerful sacramental effects of marriage and, at the same time, the contrasting values of vowed religious celibacy and marriage. It is my impression that all too often the question of the requirement of universal celibacy in the Latin Rite gets confused with a discussion about the intrinsic value of vowed religious chastity. They are distinct issues.

It is clearly the purpose of this book to offer a spiritual guide to the value, purpose, and practice of vowed Christian celibacy. I suspect that this book is a response to extremely important changes taking place in the lives of a small but fascinating group of dedicated young Christians. The following quotation from Cardinal Newman, written during the early days of the Oxford Movement (which exerted great spiritual influence on English-speaking Christians throughout the world), more than justifies the effort that Fr. Andrew has made in presenting this book:

It is, indeed, a general characteristic of the course of his providence to make the few the channels of his blessings to the many . . . . It is plain that every great change is effected by the few, not by the many; by the resolute, undaunted zealous few. One or two people, with small outward pretensions, but with their hearts in their work, these do great things. They are prepared, not by sudden excitement, or by the vague. general belief of the truth of their cause, but by deeply impressed, often repeated instructions; and since it stands to reason that it is easier to teach a few than a great number, it is plain that such people will always be few. (*Parochial and Plain Sermons*, pp. 292-293)

Fr. Andrew's words are addressed to the few. But these are a small minority spread and repeated throughout a very large multitude. This little cluster could change many things, could pass on the light in a very effective way. But they need to be encouraged and to know that they are not alone, that there are cogent answers to their critics. They need to be made aware of the powerful means given by God to help them fulfill the challenges which conscience, Divine Providence and personal religious experience have placed upon them. They need to hear clearly that this call is based on the Gospel and is reiterated down through Christian history. This is what Fr. Andrew has so ably done.

Fr. Benedict J. Groeschel, CFR

Preface

When I began writing this book, my primary concern was to offer some reflections and guidelines about celibacy as a special gift from the Lord. The inspiration came from a group of novices whom I was instructing in preparation for their First Profession. When I mentioned my growing desire to write a book on the topic of vowed chastity, they encouraged me, saying that they had seen very little in print of the material we were discussing. They felt that many people considering the priesthood or religious life would profit from the same insights they were gaining.

This encouragement became the immediate stimulus for writing this book. But as the months of writing went on, another factor of great importance increased the need for a positive approach to celibacy. That was the growing focus in the media on alleged failures of priests and religious in regard to their consecrated celibacy. There have been many accusations of sexual misconduct. Such allegations and, obviously, the actual misconduct have brought harm to its victims and scandal to the Church. This has resulted in the disedification of the faithful and a general lessening of respect for clergy and religious, especially in cases involving claims of pedophilia.

One result of this negative publicity has been a frequent call for the abolition of celibacy. Celibacy, in fact, has even been blamed as the major cause of sexual misconduct. The reasoning here, I suppose, is that if priests and religious were married, their sexual needs would be satisfied, thereby eliminating the potential for sexual misconduct. A superficial view of things might make this appear true. But on closer study, it becomes evident that this is not so. If celibacy were the primary cause of sexual misconduct, including pedophilia, then what is the cause of sexual misconduct in the case of married persons, who are not celibate? Furthermore, if we argue that celibacy should be done away with because some priests or religious fall short of their vowed commitment, then we should have to argue all the more that marriage should be done away with because a significant number of marriages end up in separation or divorce.

The main point here is simply this: Neither celibacy nor marriage is the cause of sexual misconduct; both were given by Christ to the Church. Marriage is a sacrament; celibacy is an evangelical counsel. Whatever God gives cannot be the root of evil. What is really needed is better preparation for these commitments, whether to married life or to celibate life. Focusing on celibacy, this means that those who are considering a vowed celibate life must, first of all, be better evaluated as to their general capacity and actual readiness to accept this kind of life. Our Lord emphasizes that celibacy is not for everyone (cf. Matt 19:11). Greater prudence, sensitivity to specific needs, and honesty in dealing with candidates can save a lot of frustration and pain later on.

Besides proper initial screening, vowed celibacy requires a solid teaching about the meaning, seriousness, and beauty of this evangelical counsel. As both a priest and a religious, I have always felt that vowed celibacy has been a special aspect of my commitment to Christ and to the Church. As the Servant of God Pope John Paul II constantly stressed, celibacy is at the heart of a priest's "spousal love" for Christ (which means he chooses Jesus as the special focus of his love) and then, with Christ, for the Church (which means he chooses to love and serve the members of the Lord's Mystical Body with undivided dedication). Celibacy has also been a source of personal blessings and of a unique freedom to be what I have been called to be for the sake of the kingdom of heaven! Hearing people argue that celibacy should be done away with causes me distress. After all, can our Heavenly Father no longer call individuals to this gift, in spite of the sexual license of our times? Is Jesus' teaching obsolete? Is the Holy Spirit, Who has given us the freedom of the children of God, now powerless before the demands of the flesh?

Celibacy is not an arbitrary commodity in the Catholic Church. It must be shown the honor and respect due all gifts given by her Founder, Jesus Christ. Not every priest, religious, or lay person committed privately to vowed celibacy is frustrated by it! Many have found profound joy, peace, and a unique satisfaction in their Christian call. Celibacy was given by the Holy Trinity both as a sign of the kingdom of heaven (where we will no longer marry nor be given in marriage according to our Lord's teaching in Mark 12:25), and as a gift for the sake of the kingdom of heaven (so that those called to it may use its unique freedom to serve the Lord and His people in total consecration).

It is my hope and prayer that those who read this book may grow in appreciation of celibacy as a surpassing gift of grace. Whether called to it personally or simply out of love and concern for what Christ has given to His Church in its fullness (of which celibacy is a part), may this book help in some small way to renew esteem for a wondrous part of God's mysterious working among His people.

Fr. Andrew Apostoli, CFR

Acknowledgments

I wish to express my thanks, first of all, for the spiritual. help I received while writing this book. My own prayers were directed especially to the Blessed Virgin Mary, who exemplifies in her perpetual virginity the meaning of the gift of celibacy. Not only have I learned from her example in my own life, but I have been the beneficiary of her prayerful assistance throughout the writing of this book. Then there were prayers to St. Joseph, who intercedes in a special way for those vowed to celibacy. There were also prayers to St. Thérèse of Lisieux, whose own struggles as an author I came to appreciate more and more as the task of writing this book went on. Finally, I sought the assistance of two Franciscans, St. Pio of Pietrelcina, OFM, Cap., and the Servant of God Fr. Solanus Casey, OFM, Cap., both of whom generously and joyfully lived their lives of vowed celibacy.

I also wish to thank all those who supported me by their prayers and by their words of encouragement to continue at the task.

Mindful of an old adage in the spiritual life, "Pray as if it all depends on God, but then work as if it all depends on you," I also want to acknowledge those who shared in the efforts of this task. Special thanks go to my confrere Fr. Benedict J. Groeschel, CFR, not only for his kindness in writing the foreword, but also for reviewing the manuscript and offering many valuable suggestions. I also wish to acknowledge the contributions of both Fr. Stanley Fortuna, CFR, whose research and knowledge of Greek were a great help, and of my former novice, Br. Patrick Linbeck, CFR, who initially encouraged me to write this book. Finally, I wish to thank another special person, a friend who so kindly and generously typed this book, but who asked that her name remain known to the Lord alone. May He bless her for all her time, effort and patience.

I also wish to thank Basilica Press for kindly agreeing to republish this work!

CHAPTER 1

Why Celibacy?

In a certain part of Australia there is a dirt road that runs through a canyon. The area is known for sudden changes in weather. For example, it may be raining one moment and dry the next or very hot one day and very cold the next. As a result, the dirt road has many ruts caused by cars and jeeps driving over it when it was muddy. When drivers approach this canyon a big sign greets them: "Pick your rut carefully because you're going to be in it for the next twenty miles!"

No doubt, this practical advice has helped many travelers on that dirt road in Australia. That same advice can be helpful for anyone traveling on the proverbial "road of life." This is because people face life with certain basic attitudes which express their values and convictions. Like those ruts in the canyon's dirt road, these attitudes can and will influence, and in many ways determine, everything the person does for a long time to come. This idea has special meaning for Catholics when it comes to how they view celibacy. Just as motorists were advised to pick their "rut" carefully, Catholics must carefully form their "attitude" on celibacy. Depending on one's attitude, various consequences will follow. If the attitude is positive, a life of vowed celibacy can bear much good fruit, for the Church as well as for individual celibates. On the other hand, if the attitude is negative, it can cause serious difficulties for individual Catholics, whether celibate or not.

The attitude of Catholics on this important aspect of the Church's life can be seen in response to the question, "Why celibacy?" Basically, three groups of individuals are in a position to answer this question. Hopefully, with sound teaching as a basis, their answers will provide much good for the whole community of the Church.

THOSE ALREADY COMMITTED TO CELIBACY

The first group who must answer the question "Why celibacy?" are those committed to a celibate life, whether publicly, as a priest or a religious, or privately, as a lay person. The individuals in this group have already formed their initial answer by having chosen to live celibately. However, they must continuously reanswer this question in the challenge of daily living. The joy of their religious profession day or of their diaconate ordination[1] will fade with time. Days of painful struggle will inevitably follow those days of joyful celebration. They can only remain faithful to their call by responding to the graces and inspirations of the Holy Spirit. Perseverance is possible only if celibacy grows as a positive factor in their lives. If it does not, it can easily degenerate over the years into something negative, possibly being viewed as harmful both psychologically and spiritually. In short, it is not enough to make a vow or promise of celibacy; celibates must continue to grow in their inner awareness and appreciation of this precious yet mysterious gift from God.

This explains why those already committed to celibacy must answer again, with greater insight and awareness, the question that touches the heart of their commitment: "Why celibacy?" It is not asked in order to deny celibacy or reject a commitment already made, but rather to deepen both their understanding of what they have promised the Lord and their determination to live it out faithfully. It was said of St. Bernard that he frequently asked himself a question regarding his entrance into the monastery: "Bernard, why have you come here?" He certainly did not ask that question of himself with the intention of leaving. He asked it to remind himself of his original intention for coming and to renew it with an even greater understanding and determination to become a saintly monk! St. Paul expressed a similar desire in his prayers for his converts

> And it is my prayer that your love may abound more and more, with knowledge and all discernment, so that you may approve what is excellent, and may be pure and blameless for the day of Christ (Phil 1:9-10).

THOSE DISCERNING A CALL
TO CELIBATE LIFE

The question "why celibacy?" is vital for a second group of individuals. These are the many men and women, young and not so young, who are presently considering God's call to the . priesthood or religious life, or to a private vow of celibacy. They must answer this question in the face of the secular humanist mentality prevalent in the world today. The secular humanist philosophy scoffs at the whole notion of celibacy. To the secular humanist, celibacy detaches a person from the greatest of all pleasures, namely, sexual pleasure, as well as from the many satisfactions that come with married and family life such as the experience of having children.

Even many good Catholics have become caught up in this secular humanist thinking. As a result, they pressure young people considering the priesthood or religious life and try to dissuade them. Sometimes parents will insist with their children: "I want grandchildren!" Or they may tell them (and this may come from friends as well): "Why throw away your life?" And if the person considering celibacy is especially attractive or has many promising qualities, others may sarcastically remark: "What a waste!"

In view of all this, a young man or woman. contemplating a commitment to celibacy is often under enormous pressure not to take this step. The reason for this opposition is simple. The call to celibacy can only be understood in the light of the Gospel, in the very life and teaching of Jesus Christ. It is to help those considering celibacy that this book will examine the reasons for choosing it, as well as the joys and the fulfillment that can be found in celibate life, in spite of the sacrifices such a life entails.

It is obvious that even before entering a seminary or convent potential candidates should already be attempting to live true Christian lives. This implies that they should already be making every effort to live out the virtue of chastity according to their state in life. Chastity is an essential virtue of the Christian life. Bl. Mother Teresa of Kolkata frequently said: "If there is no chastity, there is no holiness!" Chastity controls the desire for sexual pleasure and also those actions that may bring about sexual pleasure. The Church clearly recognizes that there is a form of chastity for married persons as well as for the unmarried. The *Catechism of the Catholic Church* (*CCC*) explains that:

> People should cultivate [chastity] in the way that is suited to their state of life. Some profess virginity or consecrated celibacy which enables them to give themselves to God alone with an undivided heart in a remarkable manner. Others live in the way prescribed for all by the moral law, whether they are married or single. (n. 2349)

It is surprising to come across young people considering religious life or the priesthood who seem quite unaware of the important place celibacy has in the life to which they feel called. As a result, they may enter a seminary or convent without having carefully considered its meaning.

I once dealt with a young man who had entered religious life after having spent some time in a seminary. While speaking to him about the question of celibacy, he told me that, in spite of being in a seminary environment for about three years, he had never personally embraced the call to celibacy in his heart. Rather, he had "intellectually" accepted his vocation to become a priest and religious as "the will of God." He was ready, therefore, to fulfill his vocation, including the living of celibacy, only because he felt God had called him and therefore he had a duty to live that way. As we spoke further, he revealed that if he felt he had the freedom to choose, what he really wanted was to find a young Catholic woman who shared the same ideals of the Faith as he did, marry her, and raise a large family. It was obvious that he had not seriously and personally considered celibacy! It was also obvious that because his only motivation to choose celibacy was an "obligation of duty" and not a free and loving acceptance in his heart, he should not make a commitment to celibacy, and he wisely did not.

If candidates for the religious life or the priesthood have not given enough serious consideration to the question of freely choosing celibacy in their hearts, they may find themselves entering a convent or seminary naively thinking that they can embrace such a life with little or no personal demands made upon them. Celibacy is a total life experience. It requires constant effort and sacrifice in order to faithfully live it out. But, on the other hand, the Holy Spirit bestows many joys and satisfactions on those who embrace celibacy with a free and generous love.

THE QUESTION OF CELIBACY
AND THE LAITY

In addition to those already committed by a vow of celibacy and those who are considering the choice of such a vow, a third group affected by the question "Why celibacy?" is the laity in general.2 Since priests and religious usually play a vital role in the spiritual lives of lay persons, there is a close bond between those who are committed to celibacy and those who are not. Whether it be through the administering of sacraments, teaching, or a social service ministry of one kind or another, lay men and women often look to priests and religious for help in their journey of faith. Not only do the laity look for good example from those who have committed themselves in such a public way to Christ and to the Church, but they also look for encouragement and prayerful support.

In turn, those who are committed to celibacy look to the laity for support and affirmation in the life they have chosen. This requires, therefore, that lay people understand and properly esteem the call to celibacy. Otherwise, they may put priests and religious down because of their celibate commitment, or at least question or dismiss their way of life as irrelevant. It is necessary that lay people clearly understand what a meaningful and positive gift celibacy is, both for those individuals called to live it and for the Church as a whole.

Today, many lay persons are frequently misled by media attacks against the Church's ideal of celibacy for clergy and religious. It is easy to become swept up into this misunderstanding, and become antagonistic or confused in regard to such an essential element in the lives of priests and religious. This undermines the desired unity between priests, religious, and laity in the Church who are meant to pray and work together in peaceful harmony, whether in a parish setting or on a diocesan level.

A final consideration is the helpful co-relation between

celibacy and marriage. Priests and religious look to faithful married couples who share their love with each other and their children and which also overflows to others as a source of encouragement and good example. They are keenly aware of how often married couples must make great sacrifices, deal with serious situations, or anticipate the future with great trust in God. On the other hand, married couples look to priests and religious to be faithful in their celibacy as an example of sacrifice and dedication. This, in turn, helps couples live their married vocation with greater generosity.

Hopefully, the reflections on celibacy that follow in this book will help all concerned to better esteem this gift for what it truly is: A gift from God! Celibacy seems especially needed today, when the world is so intent on the glorification of sex and sexual pleasure. When one considers the powerful witness and the positive fruits that can follow from the gift of celibacy, the question "Why celibacy?" will answer itself.

Notes

1. Diaconate ordination is the time when those men going on to the priesthood make a promise of life-long celibacy.

2. While non-clerical members of religious communities are technically laity, we will use the term "laity" and "lay people" in the popular sense, to differentiate between those who are publicly bound by a vow of celibacy and those who are not.

Chapter 2

Celibacy:
A Surpassing Gift of Grace

There is evidence of a common belief among the early Fathers of the Church that all or most of the apostles (with the clear exception of St. John) were married at the time our Lord called them to become his followers. We know, for example, that Jesus cured the mother-in-law of St. Peter (Matt 8:14-15). But this same tradition also points out that after Pentecost, the apostles, in order to live the celibacy that Jesus had lived and taught, by mutual agreement with their wives, either separated from them or lived celibately with them.[1]

At the same time, the celibacy of St. John seems to be one of the qualities that endeared him in a special way to Jesus. He is known in the Fourth Gospel as "the disciple whom Jesus loved," John was privileged to lean against the heart of Christ at the Last Supper and learn who Jesus meant when He said, "One of you will betray me" (John 13:21-26). John had the courage to stand at the Cross with Mary and was blessed to receive her as his own Mother. It is said that he received our Lady into his care, and she no doubt received him into her care (cf.

John 19:25-27). Finally, St. John the Beloved was privileged to witness the piercing of the heart of Christ, opening its treasures of love and mercy to all the world. He testifies to this in his Gospel (cf. John 19:34-37). The celibate love of this "beloved disciple" surely gave him the opportunity to be exceptionally close to Christ and His Blessed Mother.[2]

OLD TESTAMENT
EXAMPLES OF CELIBACY

What inspired the celibate commitment of the apostles was the life and teaching of our Lord. The teaching of Jesus on celibacy (cf. Matt 19:10-12) was unique and novel. Permanent celibacy is almost unheard of in the old Testament.[3]

One example we do have is the prophet Jeremiah. He was told by God not to marry and not to have any children in Jerusalem. His celibacy and childlessness were meant to be a sign to Israel, for the people had been unfaithful to God and were soon to be carried off into captivity in Babylon. As a consequence, they would become "childless." Their children would either die in battle or from disease and famine, or they would be carried off into exile (Jer 16:1-4). (It should be noted, however, that this mandatory celibacy did not seem to have made Jeremiah very happy.)

Another example of celibacy in the old Testament was also an imposed celibacy. It involved a daughter of one of the judges of Israel, a man named Jephthah (cf. Jg 11:12-31). Jephthah ruled as a chief over part of the northern kingdom of Israel. He led the Israelites into battle against the Ammonites, who were threatening to seize territory from Israel. As he went into battle, he recklessly vowed that if God helped him to defeat the Ammonites, he would sacrifice to God "whatever" came out of his house to meet him upon his return. Returning home after his victory, he was met by his daughter, his only child. When he sorrowfully told her of the vow he had made, she courageously consented to be sacrificed. She only asked her father for two months to "lament her virginity;" it seemed like a disgrace for her to die childless.[4]

These Old Testament examples of celibacy indicate that it was not understood as a blessing or a gift as much as a cause of childlessness, It was to be endured either as a trial, as in the case of Jeremiah, or as a tragedy, as in the case of the daughter of Jephthah.

NEW TESTAMENT EXAMPLES
OF CELIBACY

Only when we come to the New Testament do we see celibacy as a positive gift of God. Our Lady is the first example we meet. Her celibate virginity is reflected in her words to the Archangel Gabriel, who appeared to her at the Annunciation (Luke 1:26-38). When Gabriel addressed Mary as the highly favored daughter of God, "full of grace," he told her that she would bear a Son. Mary responded to the Angel, saying, "How can this be since I do not know man?" (Luke 1:34, *NAB*).

At the time of the Annunciation Mary was betrothed to St. Joseph[5] Therefore, her question is most important. It tells us that not only was Mary not yet living with St. Joseph as husband and wife during this time of their solemn engagement, but it further implies that even after her marriage to him, she did not intend to use her rights as a married woman. She would not engage in a sexual relationship with St. Joseph; she would remain a virgin even after marriage. Otherwise, her question would make no sense. If she had intended to use her marriage rights, she would have realized that she would conceive a son when she began to live with St. Joseph. Her question implies that she had not yet been with him in physical intimacy, and she did not intend, even after her marriage, to use her marital rights.

The Fathers of the Church felt that the question asked by Mary implied that she had already been inspired to consecrate her virginity permanently to God. This is also the only logical conclusion we can draw.[6] Such a consecration would have been inspired in her by the Holy Spirit as a way to dedicate her whole life fully to God. In so doing, she would have forsaken any natural hope of becoming the mother of the promised Messiah. However, one may fittingly conclude that the deep faith and generous love that moved Mary to consecrate her virginity to God was inspired precisely in view of her having been chosen to be the Mother of the Son of God. Our Lady was truly "blessed among women," she through whom the Word would take flesh and dwell among us!

The constant tradition of the Catholic Church also teaches that Jesus was celibate. There is no direct reference to this in the Gospel accounts,[7] but they do indicate that His example of chastity was beyond reproach. His enemies, especially the Pharisees, accused Him of many wrongdoings, such as not observing the Sabbath rest and not observing ritual washings before eating, but they never dared to accuse Him of any sexual wrongdoing. His conduct was beyond all doubt or suspicion. It is chiefly from the Lord's teaching on celibacy, however, that we assume He observed it.

Christ's Teaching on Celibacy

Our Lord presented His teaching on celibacy in the context of speaking about the permanence of marriage (cf. Matt 19:3-12). Jesus was asked by the Pharisees whether or not a man can divorce his wife for any reason. He responds by telling them that a married couple are no longer two but one flesh, and that no one can separate what God has thus joined together; He outlaws divorce. As a result, the apostles respond: "If that is the case between man and wife, it is better not to marry" (Matt

19:10). In response to their remark, Jesus sets forth His teaching on celibacy:

> Not all men can receive this saying, but only those to whom it is given. For there are eunuchs who have been so from birth, and there are eunuchs who have been made eunuchs by men, and there are eunuchs who have made themselves eunuchs for the sake of the kingdom of heaven. He who is able to receive this, let him receive it. (Matt 19:11-12)

Our Lord here indicates that His followers will have another choice besides marriage as a way of life. It will be the way of dedicated celibacy. But he tells them that this is not a teaching meant for all. He indicates that many will be unable to "receive" (grasp and appreciate) this teaching or will lack the generous will needed to "receive" (accept and embrace) it.[8]

As we have seen, the apostles took this teaching of Christ seriously. After the Ascension and the coming of the Holy Spirit on Pentecost, they separated by mutual agreement from their wives, or at least lived celibately with them.[9] The apostles no doubt embraced celibacy in order to follow Christ's personal example as well as to fully live His teaching on this point.

St. Paul's Exhortation to Celibacy

The great Apostle, St. Paul, also stressed this teaching.[10] We find it especially in his First Letter to the Corinthians. Speaking of marriage and celibacy, St. Paul says that he had chosen celibacy for himself and he wanted others to choose it as well. He recognized, however, that God calls some to marriage and others to celibacy, and he respected the freedom of God's call and the freedom of his readers' choice. He puts it this way:

> I wish that all were as I myself am. But each has his own special gift from God, one of one kind and one of another. To the unmarried and the widows, I say that it is well for them to

remain single as I do. (1 Cor 7:7-8)

In his teaching, St. Paul clearly recognizes that each person is called to their own particular gift, whether that be celibacy or marriage. He even expresses his concern that someone choosing celibacy might lack the self-control or discipline needed to live it faithfully. He likewise goes on to stress the contrast between unmarried persons whose hearts remain "undivided" in serving the Lord and their neighbor, and married persons who are "divided" in their love and service of God and their spouse.[11]

CELIBACY AMONG THE EARLY CHRISTIANS

In the fervor of their faith, the first generations of Christians embraced celibacy as a means to imitate Christ more closely and to give Him their undivided service. The memory of Christ was fresh in the minds of these earliest Christians. In their deep love for Him, they sought to imitate Him as closely as possible. This imitation of Christ was the goal of Christian life.

It was felt that the greatest way to imitate Christ was through martyrdom. After all, Jesus had said that there can be no greater love than to lay down one's life for one's friends (John 15:13). As Jesus had given Himself, the early Christians wanted to give themselves totally through martyrdom. Furthermore, by martyrdom they were assured of their salvation, for the Lord had said: "For whoever would save his life will lose it, and whoever loses his life for My sake will find it" (Matt 16:25).

As they awaited the opportunity for martyrdom, many of the early Christians embraced celibacy as a closer imitation of Christ. It was seen as one of the main ascetical practices of the early Christians.[12] Like St. Paul, who said that he carried about in his body every day the "dying" of Christ, so celibate persons, by trying to remain faithful to their commitment, carry the "dying" of Christ in a special way within them: dying to their passions and to the allurements of the flesh.

As time went on and the persecutions stopped, Christian men and women, in great numbers, began to live celibate lives in their own homes, celibacy being embraced as a kind of private consecration. Others left the cities and towns and went out into wilderness areas, living in solitary desert hermitages in Egypt, Palestine, and Syria. These men and women became known as the desert "fathers" and "mothers."

Eventually, those consecrated to celibacy began to gather into communities for mutual support, both for their material needs and for spiritual encouragement. Still later, these communities of consecrated men and women were given official recognition by the local bishop. Some of them adopted various "rules of life" and began to wear a distinctive garb to indicate their consecrated state as celibates.

CELIBACY IN RELIGIOUS LIFE
AND THE PRIESTHOOD

In due time, celibacy became an essential element for those who embraced the religious life. Interestingly, in the Benedictine monastic tradition, which dominated religious life in the Christian west for about seven hundred years, there was no explicit vow of celibacy. The three Benedictine vows were of obedience, conversion of life, and stability. However, the evangelical counsels of celibacy and poverty were implied in the life of the Benedictine monks and nuns. These monks and nuns were considered as "minors" who had no rights of their own. The abbot or abbess of the monastery was seen as the adult figure. A "minor," according to ancient Roman household custom, needed the permission of the adult parent to marry and to own property. Thus, the idea of celibacy (not being married) and poverty (not owning anything) were implied in the life of a monk or nun living in voluntary submission to the superior.

From the twelfth and thirteenth centuries, when new forms of religious life emerged in great numbers (e.g., the mendicant orders, such as the Franciscans, Dominicans, Carmelites), a vow of chastity, along with the now familiar vows of poverty and obedience, were almost universally taken by religious. Certain communities sometimes even added an additional vow, usually in connection with a specific aspect of their life or work.[13]

Celibacy for priests was encouraged in the early centuries and its practice was widespread, especially in the Western Church (Latin rite). It eventually became a universal obligation for all priests in the West.[14] The practice of celibacy for all priests of the Latin rite was clearly reiterated by the Second Vatican Council and by other ecclesial documents since then.[15] The Eastern rites, on the other hand, have maintained the tradition of allowing married men to be ordained;[16] however, they have also maintained the tradition of choosing their bishops only from among the celibate clergy or monks.

VATICAN II AND CELIBACY

During Vatican Council II (1960-1964) the Church, through its bishops, gathered together under the leadership of Popes John XXIII and Paul VI. Enlightened by the Holy Spirit, the Council looked at the life of the Church in itself and in relation to the modern world. The most important document that the Council produced was the *Dogmatic Constitution on the Church* (*Lumen Gentium*), issued November 21, 1964. In this document, the Church presented her own inner structure and life, focusing on both the "hierarchy" and the "laity."[17] In Chapter 5, "The Call to Holiness," the Second Vatican Council stressed that all Catholics, whether they be clerical members or lay members of the Church, are called to the fullness of holiness:

> All in the Church, whether they belong to the hierarchy or are cared for, by it, are called to holiness, according to the Apostle's saying: "For this is the will of God, your sanctification" (I Thes 4:3). This holiness of the Church is constantly shown forth in the fruits of grace which the Spirit produces in the faithful and so it must be; it is expressed in many ways by the individuals who, each in his own state of life, tend to the perfection of love, thus sanctifying others . . . . It is therefore quite clear that all Christians, in any state or walk of life, are called to the fullness of Christian life and to the perfection of love . . . . (*Lumen Gentium*, Ch. 5)

In the same chapter, the document speaks of two exceptional signs of holiness. The first of these is martyrdom, which involves the total giving of one's self to Almighty God. The document states:

> Since Jesus, the Son of God, showed his love by laying down his life for us, no one has greater love than he who lays down his life for him and for his brothers. Some Christians have been called from the beginning and will always be called to give this greatest testimony of love to all, especially to persecutors. Martyrdom makes the disciple like his Master, who willingly accepted death for the salvation of the world and, through it, he is conformed to him by the shedding of blood. Therefore, the Church considers it the highest gift and the supreme test of love. (*Ibid.*, Ch. 5)

But immediately after emphasizing martyrdom as the supreme sign of love, *Lumen Gentium* points to a second exceptional sign of holiness: living out the evangelical counsels of poverty, chastity, and obedience. The Church sees this sign lived out by those Christians who freely respond to and observe the evangelical counsels, which Christ proposed to the disciples in the Gospel. Among these Gospel counsels, "celibacy for the sake of the kingdom of heaven" holds first place. This is what the Council teaches about celibacy:

> Towering among these counsels is that precious gift of divine grace given to some by the Father to devote themselves to God alone more easily with an undivided heart in virginity or celibacy. This perfect continence for love of the kingdom of heaven has always been held in high esteem by the Church as a sign and stimulus of love, and as a singular source o f spiritual fertility in the world. (*Ibid.* Ch. 6)

The Second Vatican Council sees celibacy for the sake of the kingdom of heaven as a surpassing gift of grace.[18] It is given by the Father, and it anticipates in a mysterious way the life of the kingdom of heaven. Jesus says that those who are in the kingdom will neither marry nor be given in marriage (cf. Matt 22:30). Celibacy is esteemed, then, as a sign pointing to the life beyond this world.[19] By it, celibates forfeit the joys and satisfactions of married life in order to give themselves more completely to the work of the kingdom of God here on earth.

The Council tells us that embracing celibacy is a sign and stimulus of Christian love as well as a source of spiritual fruitfulness in the Church. We shall next examine what the relationship is between celibacy and Christian love, and how to make the choice of celibacy with greater love, freedom and spiritual fruitfulness.

Notes

1. For a full and interesting treatment of this question, see Christian Cochini, SJ, *Apostolic Origins of Priestly Celibacy*, Ch. 4, "The Issue of the Apostles' Marriages" (Ignatius Press: San Francisco, 1993), pp. 65-83.

2. Two testimonies to this effect by early Fathers of the Church (as quoted in *ibid.* pp. 68-69) are Epiphanius (d. 403 AD) and St. Jerome (d. 419 or 420):

> If Jesus, as he was dying on the Cross, entrusted Him mother to John and not to Peter or any other

Apostle, it was because John was a virgin. (*Panarion* [*Adversus Haereses*] *Haer.* 78, 10. PG 42, 174c.)

and,

> Yet John, one of the disciples who was said to be the youngest among the apostles, and whose faith in Christ started when he was a virgin, remained a virgin, and this is the reason that he was preferred by the Lord and leaned on Jesus' breast. (*Adversus Jovinianum*, I, 26. PL 23, 246b—c.)

3. There were a number of periods of temporary celibacy referred to in the Old Testament. For example, when Moses was about to receive the commandments from God, he admonished the people to prepare for the event by abstaining from sexual relations. The same was required of priests during the time of their liturgical service. Finally, temporary celibacy was demanded of King David and his soldiers by the high priest Abimelech when, hungry and lacking their own provisions, the soldiers needed to eat the sacred bread in the temple.

There is also evidence that in the period just before the coming of Christ, a community of Jewish people living near the Dead Sea, known as the "Essenes" or "Qumran monks," observed celibacy. Their founder, the "Teacher of Righteousness," seemed to favor celibacy for the original members of the Essene community. The exact motive for this celibacy is not certain. Possible reasons were: (1) to attain complete liturgical purity; (2) to prepare for the final spiritual battle since they sensed that the end times were near; and (3) belief that married life would divide the monks' allegiance to the community and so could threaten to break up the community.

4. In biblical times, bearing a child was seen as a blessing from the Lord. For example, in Psalm 128, we read that one of the blessings given by the Lord to a man who fears Him is that his wife will be like a fruitful vine and his children will be like shoots of the olive tree around his table, and that he will see his

children's children in a happy Jerusalem!

5. In ancient times, the Jewish practice of marriage involved the couple first being betrothed or solemnly engaged for one year, during which time they lived apart and not as husband and wife. At the end of that year, the husband would go to the house of his bride-to-be, take her to his home, and there they would celebrate their wedding festival for about one week with family and friends.

6. A summary of the Church's teaching on Mary's perpetual virginity is presented in the book *Theotokos: A Theological Encyclopedia of the Blessed Virgin Mary*, by Michael O'Carroll, CSSp (Michael Glazier, Inc., Wilmington, DE, 1982, pp. 363-364):

> From the time of St. Gregory of Nyssa in the East and of St. Augustine in the West, the opinion has been held that Mary's reply to the angel, "How shall this be since I know not a man" (Luke 1:34) meant that she had the intention, though married to Joseph, of remaining a virgin. "The angel," says St. Gregory, "announces offspring; but she cleaves to her virginity preferring her [bodily] integrity to what the angel manifests. She neither lacks faith in the angel nor departs from her promise. . . . Because she was bound to preserve her flesh, which was consecrated to God as a sacred gift, untouched, therefore she says 'though you are an angel, though you come from heaven, though what is shown is beyond human nature, it is nevertheless impossible for me to know man.'" St. Augustine wrote: "Before He was conceived, He chose to be born of a woman already consecrated to God. This is the meaning of the words with which Mary replied to the angel's message that she was to bear a child ('How shall this be. . .'). Surely she would not say that unless she had previously vowed her virginity to God (*nisi Deo virginem se ante*

vovisset). But because the customs of the Jews still refused this [her vow of virginity], she was betrothed to a just man, who would not take her by violence but rather guard against the violent what she had vowed."

Another author, Fr. Valentine Long, OFM, in his book *The Mother of God* (Franciscan Herald Press, Chicago, 1967), says that Mary made a vow of perpetual virginity to Almighty God. He says that vows were frequently taken for various reasons by the Israelites in biblical times. Commenting on St. Luke's narrative of the Annunciation and specifically of our Lady's words to the angel that she "did not know man," the author says this:

> The text unmistakably shows her (Mary's) mind already made up to forego the sexual privileges of a wife by the time the angel invited her to be a different kind of mother. She was not indifferent to the honor (of motherhood). Her eventual acceptance proves she was not, once the angel had solved her difficulty. Simply, having given the Lord her solemn word, she could not, in conscience, feel free to go back on it. Her familiarity with the sacred writings of her people would, of itself, constrain her . . . from all of which, it is reasonable, quite as much as traditional, to conclude that at their betrothal, Joseph agreed to Mary's condition and was himself in favor of a virginal marriage. No other interpretation can bring sense out of the facts .... (*Ibid.*, p. 44)

7. Some Scripture scholars have suggested that when Jesus asked the apostles who the people thought He was, and they answered that some people thought He was the prophet Jeremiah, this was because of the striking similarity of celibacy. It has been pointed out how unique Jeremiah's celibacy was in the Old Testament. Normally, when rabbis traveled around

teaching, they brought not only a group of disciples, but then wives as well. Since Our Lord did not travel around with a wife, His practice of celibacy would have stood out clearly for this reason.

8. We shall look at the teaching of Jesus regarding celibacy more closely in Chapter 3.

9. Interestingly, in the life of Mahatma Gandhi, the great religious leader of the Hindu people in India, he and his wife separated, or at least refrained from a sexual relationship. He had approached her saying that he needed to practice celibacy as a means of deepening his own religious dedication and mission among the people.

10. In regard to St. Paul, there was some controversy among the early Fathers of the Church as to whether or not he was ever married (a widower) or was still married at the time of his conversion or whether he was always single (unmarried). In any case, all agreed that he lived celibately, whether as a widower or still married or as always single. See Christian Cochini, SJ, op. cit., pp. 74-77.

11. We shall look more closely at this teaching of St. Paul in the following chapter.

12. The word "ascetical" comes from the Greek word askesis, which means the efforts made in learning an art or a discipline, such as a soldier in drilling for war or an athlete in practicing and preparing for competition. The early Christian celibates considered themselves as "ascetics" who were striving, like St. Paul, to run the race and fight the good fight to obtain the crown of eternal life (cf. 2 Tim 4:7-8). Gradually, other "ascetical" practices such as fasting and works of mercy were added to the celibate's life.

13. The Missionaries of Charity, founded by Bl. Mother Teresa of Kolkata, take a fourth vow "to give free and wholehearted service to the poorest of the poor." The Jesuits take a fourth vow of obedience to the Pope. The Passionists take a fourth vow of special love and devotion to the passion

of Christ, promising to spread that devotion in every possible way.

14. For a full presentation of the history of priestly celibacy, see Christian Cochini, SJ, *op. cit.*

15. The teaching of the Second Vatican Council is found in its decree *Presbyterorum Ordinis*, n. 16. Some recent significant documents are (1) Pope Paul VI, in his encyclical letter, *Sacerdotalis Coelibatus*, June 24, 1967, n. 14; (2) Pope John Paul II, in his post-synodal apostolic exhortation, *Pastores Dabo Vobis*, n. 29; and (3) *Code of Canon Law*, Canon 277, n. 1.

Another document which gives a summary of the Church's renewed pledge to maintain clerical celibacy is the *Directory for the Life and Ministry of Priests.* Prepared by the Congregation for the Clergy, it was approved by Pope John Paul II on January 31, 1994. It states:

> Convinced of the profound theological and pastoral motives upholding the relationship between celibacy and the priesthood, and enlightened by the testimony which confirms to this day, in spite of painful negative cases, its spiritual and evangelical validity, the Church has reaffirmed in Vatican Council II and repeatedly in teachings of the Pontifical Magisterium the "firm will to maintain the law which requires celibacy freely chosen and perpetual for candidates to priestly ordination in the Latin rite." (Pope John Paul II, *Pastores*, n. 29). Celibacy, in fact, is a gift which the Church has received and desires to retain, convinced that it is a good for the Church itself and for the world. (*Directory*, n. 57)

16. However, they observe the practice of not allowing men to marry after they have been ordained, nor of allowing married priests to remarry if their spouse dies.

17. In Chapter 3, the *Constitution* focuses on the

hierarchy. This chapter includes reflections on the unique role of the Pope as bishop of Rome, the other bishops (both individually and as a college), priests and their duties, and finally, deacons and their roles within the Church community.

Chapter 4 of the *Constitution* focuses on the laity. It discusses their vital membership in the Church and how each baptized person shares in the roles of Christ as Priest (a call to worship), Prophet (a call to witness to the truths of our Catholic Faith), and King (a call to serve as Jesus served) in the "Priesthood of all the Faithful."

18. This idea of the Second Vatican Council that celibacy is a "gift" is brought out clearly also in Canon Law:

> Clerics are obliged to observe perfect and perpetual continence for the sake of the kingdom of heaven and therefore are obliged to observe celibacy, which is a special gift of God, by which sacred ministers can adhere more easily to Christ with an undivided heart and can more freely dedicate themselves to the service of God and humankind (Canon 277, n. 1).

19. This is referred to as the eschatological dimension of celibacy, from the Greek word *eschata*, meaning the last things or the end times. It refers to the fact that celibacy anticipates, here and now on earth, the unmarried aspect of the saints in heaven for all eternity.

CHAPTER 3

Celibacy: A Sign of Love

SECULAR HUMANISM
REJECTS CELIBACY

Many people today, both inside and outside the Church, do not see celibacy as a surpassing gift of God to His people. This can be attributed to many factors.

We have already noted the extent to which society is characterized by secular humanism and values which basically reject God's plan and purpose. This secular attitude has made sex into an idol. We live in an era following the "sexual revolution" of the late 1960s and early 1970s. This revolution undermined many basic Christian principles and values that had traditionally formed at least the public attitude toward sexual morality in American and Western European society. In place of these traditional. values, we now find ourselves in a neo-pagan society in which sexual pleasure has become the "be all" and the "end all" of life. Obviously, in such a godless society, celibacy not only seems out of date, but it appears totally out of touch with secular reality. However, it is precisely for this reason that people who are celibate have enormous power as witnesses of Christ and the Gospel values. They are clear "signs of contradiction" against the distorted emphasis that our neo-pagan society places on sex today.

MEDIA PERSECUTION ATTEMPTS
TO DISCREDIT CELIBACY

Celibacy has been further discredited by a deliberate attack against the Catholic Church in the public media. This persecution seems to stem from the major role the Church plays in guarding traditional Judaeo-Christian moral values. Because the Church condemns practices like abortion (as the killing of innocent unborn children) and homosexual activity (as contrary to God's law), the media, which overwhelmingly support both these forms of immoral behavior, have made it a point to publicize the failures of priests and religious in regard to their commitment to celibacy.

Such persecution of the Church by its contemporary society is not new. For example, we have evidence of it in a document dating all the way back to the first Christian century. It is known as *A Letter to Diognetus*. It describes the persecution which Christians of that time were experiencing and presents some possible reasons why:

> Christians are indistinguishable from other men either by nationality, language or customs. . . Yet there is something extraordinary about their lives. They live in their own countries as though they were only passing through. They play their full role as citizens, but labor under all the disabilities of aliens. Any country can be their homeland, but for them, their homeland, wherever it may be, is a foreign country. Like others, they marry and have children, but they do not expose them. They share their meals, but not their

wives. They live in the flesh, but they are not governed by the desires of the flesh. They pass their days upon earth, but they are citizens of heaven. Obedient to the laws, they yet live on a level that transcends the law.

Christians love all men, but all men persecute them. Condemned because they are not understood, they are put to death, but raised to life again. They live in poverty, but enrich many. They are totally destitute, but possess an abundance of everything. They suffer dishonor, but that is their glory. They are defamed, but vindicated. A blessing is their answer to abuse, deference their response to insult. For the good they do, they receive the punishment of malefactors, but even then they rejoice, as though receiving the gift of life. They are attacked by the Jews as aliens, they are persecuted by the Greeks; yet no one can explain the reason for this hatred.

To speak in general terms, we may say that the Christian is to the world what the soul is to the body. . . . The body hates the soul and wars against it, not because of any injury the soul has done it, but because of the restriction the soul places on its pleasures. Similarly, the world hates the Christians, not because they have done it any wrong, but because they are opposed to its enjoyments. (nos. 5-6)

Such persecution should not surprise those committed to Christ. At the Last Supper (John 15:19), the Lord warned us that if we belonged to the world, the world would love us, but because He has called us to follow Him and to put aside the values of the world and embrace His own, the world hates us. The media publicize the failures of priests and religious in order to diminish the respect in which they are held. This has led to a general decline in the esteem with which people recognize celibacy as a surpassing gift of the Holy Spirit.

MANY SECULAR PSYCHOLOGISTS BELITTLE CELIBACY

One final factor adding to the loss of esteem for celibacy

are the claims of many modern psychologists who hold that celibacy is impossible to live or, at best, unhealthy.

For example, they maintain that it destroys personal growth and responsibility. But this observation does not apply any more to celibates than to married persons. Either or both can equally shirk their personal responsibilities. True psychological growth requires a growth in love and inner freedom. Celibacy can uniquely help to develop these qualities in an individual. When lived for the right motives and according to authentic moral norms, it can lead to a deepening of an individual's personal life and psychological growth just as much as marriage can.

Another claim some psychologists make is that celibates do not share intimacy with anyone else. While this may seem obvious at first glance, it is not a true picture. It is true that a celibate does not share his or her life intimately with another person in a physical or sexual way, but their life is shared deeply with many people by heartfelt caring, by the sharing of time, gifts, and possessions, and in true, enduring friendships

Celibacy for the sake of the kingdom of heaven, by its very nature as a call from God, is not a freedom from responsibilities, but a freedom to live more fully and generously for others. Celibates have, as St. Paul said, that "undivided heart" by which they can give themselves more completely to the love and service of God and of their neighbor. The Second Vatican Council addressed this point in *Lumen Gentium*:

> Let us realize that while the profession of the evangelical counsels involves the renunciation of goods that undoubtedly deserve to be highly valued, it does not constitute an obstacle to the true development of the human person but by its nature is supremely beneficial to that development. For the counsels, when willingly embraced in accordance with each one's personal vocation, contribute in no small degree to the purification of the heart and to spiritual freedom: they continually stimulate one to ardor in the life of love; and

above all, they have the power to conform the Christian more fully to that kind of poor and virginal life which Christ, the Lord, chose for himself and which his Virgin Mother also embraced. (*LG, op. cit.*, p. 406)

CELIBACY AND CHRISTIAN LOVE

To understand the connection between love and celibacy, we should recall the teaching of the Second Vatican Council cited in the last chapter, that celibacy for the sake of the kingdom of heaven has always been held in high esteem by the Church as both a "sign" and a "stimulus" of love. Let us now examine the first of these aspects of celibacy.

Celibacy can be called a "sign" of love because of the generosity needed to surrender or forsake the joys and pleasures of married life (cf. Matt 19:10-12). Our Lord said that it was not a teaching that everyone could accept. This implies that there will be some who cannot understand, appreciate or acknowledge the importance of celibacy, much less have the generous love needed to accept it in their own lives. Instead, it can only be appreciated and embraced by those to whom it is given; it is truly a grace, a free gift from God. Our Lord's teaching stresses this point. We could paraphrase Jesus' words, as I once heard it expressed: "Let the one with generous love to accept this teaching, let that person embrace it" (cf. Matt 19:12).

An important question to answer is: "Why does embracing celibacy require a generous love?" The answer is quite simple. It is because in embracing celibacy, persons renounce experiences which touch deeply upon their psycho-sexual nature as human beings. Let us look at three of these renunciations and how a person committed to celibacy must deal with them.

RENUNCIATION OF INTIMATE
COMPANIONSHIP

The first experience that is renounced in celibacy is that of the unique intimate companionship that characterizes marriage, which today often is referred to as marital intimacy.[1] It was God who said: "It is not good for the man to be alone. I will make a suitable partner for him" (Gen 2:18). As human beings, we experience a desire for the love and affection of "someone very special." We feel a strong desire to have someone share our lives, with its joys and sorrows, hopes and disappointments, successes, and failures. This desire for intimacy and affection is uniquely fulfilled in marriage in the love of husband and wife. How true it is that because of the unique and intimate love that unites them, from their two lives, they now form one!

Celibate persons, by renouncing the special intimacy and companionship of a spouse, experience a void in their lives. It is important that this void not become a negative factor. From time to time the celibate person will also experience a sense of loneliness sometimes described as the experience of the absence of another person's special presence or support. But there are, helps that can turn this loneliness into an opportunity for positive growth.

The danger of loneliness becoming a negative experience can be avoided by the positive gift of prayerful solitude. The uniquely "undivided heart" of the celibate person provides a blessed opportunity for a more open and deeper relationship with God. The void or aloneness that celibate persons experience can become an opportunity to deepen their relationship to God through constant prayer. St. Paul, in his teaching on celibacy, says that even a married couple may separate from one another for a time for the sake of prayer (1 Cor 7:5). Prayer is one of the strongest means of sustaining a life of faithful celibacy.

Another means to turn loneliness into positive growth is found in self-giving relationships to others. This refers primarily to family and friends with whom the celibate person shares necessary human affirmation, such as feelings of acceptance, understanding, encouragement and the like. In a unique way, those called to religious life or the priesthood will meet the need for affectivity in friendships with fellow religious or priests with whom they live and work and share life.[2]

RENUNCIATION OF SEXUAL PLEASURES

Those who commit themselves to celibacy also freely renounce the sexual pleasures and satisfactions proper to a marital relationship. These are probably the most intense physical pleasures that human beings experience. They have an enormously strong attraction because of our psycho-sexual makeup. In order to hold these strong attractions and impulses in check, the celibate person must develop a sense of discipline and self-control. This can only be achieved by the grace and power of the Holy Spirit, who produces in us the fruits of chastity, modesty, and continency.

Celibate persons must learn to inwardly renounce these strong sexual pleasures and attractions. This is an important point not only for perseverance in the celibate commitment, but also in order for one's life to be lived with a certain measure of joy, peace and inner freedom. This means that the celibate person must not constantly look back at those pleasures and satisfactions they have surrendered, wishing or desiring them once again. What our Lord said of living the Christian life in general can apply in particular to this aspect of living a celibate life: "No one who puts his hand to the plow and looks back is fit for the kingdom of God" (Luke 9:62).

Our Lord is telling us that once we begin our course in life, we must not keep looking back to what we have given up or we will forget the direction we have chosen to move in, do a poor job at the task begun (like plowing crooked furrows), and ultimately slow down and possibly block all progress along the way chosen. If a married person, for example, keeps looking back with curiosity or regret at an old girlfriend or boyfriend they used to date, he or she will hardly have a happy and satisfying marriage. Likewise, the celibate person who keeps looking back with regret to the pleasures and satisfactions of married life will hardly find deep peace, joy or fulfillment in the celibacy they have embraced for the sake of the kingdom of heaven.

The Servant of God Archbishop Fulton J. Sheen once offered the following advice, which hits at the heart of the attitude of those celibates who want to find peace and fulfillment in their lives: "By our celibacy we must learn to live with a mystery in ourselves." To understand the full import of these words, we should keep in mind that the biblical Hebrew word for expressing sexual relationships was the verb "to know." For example, we read that Adam "knew" his wife, Eve (cf. Gen 4:1). This does not mean that he knew who she was, but rather that, through their sexual relationship, they experienced a unique knowledge of one another. This knowledge, when rooted in true Christian love and flowing from mutual acceptance, respect, and self-donation, is most complete between husband and wife. In marriage, there is a knowledge or experience of one another that is physically, emotionally, and spiritually fulfilling.

Celibate persons, on the other hand, will not "know" (that is, "experience") this unique and mysterious knowledge. Therefore, they live with an unexplored "mystery" deep within themselves. In their commitment to God for the sake of the kingdom, celibates must freely but faithfully surrender the attraction and the strong curiosity to know this sexual mystery. By guarding their thoughts and desires, their actions and the use of their senses, as well as the affections of their hearts, they dispose themselves to live the celibate life in a free, peacefilled and joyful way. This determined self-discipline is one of the deciding factors between a positive rather than a negative, or a joyful rather than a depressed experience of celibate living. St. Paul reminds us of our frailty in trying to live out our lives as Christians: "But we have this treasure in earthen vessels, to show that the transcendent power belongs to God and not to us" (2 Cor 4:7).

The treasure that the celibate possesses is the gift of an undivided heart, now consecrated in a unique way to God. It is God who gives the grace to remain faithful in body, mind, and heart to the total commitment that celibacy entails; it can only be sustained by the grace and inspiration of the Holy Spirit. He is the source of our surpassing power, while our own frailty is like that of earthen vessels.

RENUNCIATION OF ONE'S OWN CHILDREN

The third great renunciation which a celibate person makes is that of having his or her own children. The desire to be a parent is deep in each person. It is generally presumed that this desire is stronger in women than in men, but at some moment in life, almost everyone will experience a desire for children of one's own. This is especially felt when the celibate person is with other family members and friends who have children. This can become a source of particular difficulty for women as they approach the period of mid-life when the physical possibility of having children is passing by.

In this renunciation of one's own children, one must realize the need to reach out to others in service. Such service can entail meeting the physical or material needs of others, such as providing food and clothing or assisting with the intellectual needs of others through teaching or in training others; or one can serve the spiritual needs of others, especially through teaching people about the Catholic Faith and leading them closer to God.

By their calling, celibates must not destroy their creative potential to "parent" others. A man must not, because of his celibate commitment, annihilate his potential to be a "father" to others any more than a woman must repress all sense of her potential for being a "mother." This would deny something of one's humanness. Rather, their creative energies must be redirected or "sublimated" to higher goals. This is especially true for religious and priests who, through their ministry, whether active or contemplative, assist others in coming to true life in Christ. These are truly "spiritual children," sons and daughters in Christ.

St. Paul refers to his own spiritual children when he writes:

> I do not write this to make you ashamed, but to admonish you as my beloved children. For though you have countless guides in Christ, you do not have many fathers. For I became your father in Christ Jesus through the Gospel. (1 Cor 4:14-15)

Many of the saints, in their zeal for the work of God, were quite conscious of having brought forth "spiritual children" through their work and prayer for others. This was a way of fulfilling their desire for children in fidelity to their celibate commitment. Though physically having no children of one's own, a certain spiritual fruitfulness is part of every celibate's authentic life in Christ. The celibate resembles our Blessed Lady who, though a perpetual virgin, is so unique that she not only brings forth Christ spiritually in her heart but even physically in her womb. The Virgin Mary is, in a unique way, the perfect model of spiritual parenting and spiritual fruitfulness for the Christian celibate person.

SURRENDERING THE "IDEAL MARRIAGE"

It is very important for celibates to bear in mind the fact that when they surrender the three significant joys and pleasures associated with marriage, namely, intimacy, sexual pleasure, and children of their own, they always do so in the offering of an "ideal" marriage situation. It must be recognized, however, that many married couples, in spite of these pleasures and joys, struggle to remain faithful to their marital commitment. Many couples practice virtue in their married lives under the most adverse circumstances, remaining faithful to God and to one another through trial and even tragedy. Such virtue is often heroic. But when the celibate renounces marriage, he or she surrenders to God the best possible marriage with all the fulfillment that he or she might have experienced. Celibate surrender involves the very best one could give. Therefore, only love can be the authentic "sign" for the celibate embracing his or her gift for the sake of the kingdom of heaven.

Notes

1. I recognize that various authors use the word "intimacy" to mean very different things. Many speak of a celibate's need for "intimacy." However, I am using the word in a much more restricted sense. What some writers refer to as "celibate intimacy," I prefer to include under friendship and the need for affective maturity. My reasoning is that the term "intimacy" has a connotation that can easily mislead individuals into depths of a relationship that may prove to be far more intense than they can deal with chastely. This is especially true in the case of those who are young in age or who have not developed sufficient affective maturity.

By "intimacy," then, I mean the unique bonding of persons that can only legitimately be experienced in the permanence and exclusiveness of a marital relationship. It expresses the "two become one" effect of marriage, with a complete union expressed on all levels: physical, emotional, and spiritual. By this very definition, it excludes a person in consecrated celibacy. However, the celibate retains his or her need for affection, affirmation, belonging, and the like. These needs are fulfilled by such means as personal friendship, religious community living, collaboration in ministry, and family ties, all of which possess, to a greater or lesser degree, certain characteristics of "intimacy."

2. We shall look at these means of sustaining celibate life in greater detail in Chapters I I and 12.

CHAPTER 4

Celibacy: A Stimulus to Love

The Second Vatican Council calls celibacy a stimulus to
love. This is because fidelity to a celibate commitment demands
constant, loving dedication over the years. This, in turn, requires
that the celibate person develop a positive attitude about chastity,
recognizing how it affects body, mind, and heart. Let us look at
these three aspects more closely.

CHASTE IN BODY

Celibate persons must be chaste in body. This means
they renounce any directly sexual or genital actions in their own
body or with the body of another person. This implies that they
recognize, in a unique way, St. Paul's teaching that the body is
both a ". . . member of Christ. . ." and a ". . .temple of the Holy
Spirit, . . ." who dwells within us, and that we must bear and
glorify God within our bodies (1 Cor 6:19-20). He tells us that
the body is not for immorality but for the Lord. By baptism,
our body is spiritually united to Christ and destined to share

with our soul in Jesus' glory in heaven. Sexual immorality sins against the body and defiles it, both as a member of Christ and as a temple of the Holy Spirit. Physical chastity is at the very heart of the celibate commitment because the celibate person renounces those sexual acts[1] that are uniquely at the center of married life.

Along with being chaste in their actions, celibate persons must also foster modesty[2] in the use of their bodily senses. Left unguarded, our senses can receive stimuli which arouse feelings of sexual pleasure. For example, allowing oneself to view immodest pictures or pornographic movies would likely result in reactions of sexual pleasure, along with strong sexual attractions and desires. Such stimuli would prove to be a moral danger. Celibate persons, therefore, must keep prudent custody over their eyes as well as their other senses so as to avoid those things which would unduly stir up strong sexual feelings, thereby placing themselves into situations in which they could transgress their commitment to God.

CHASTE IN MIND

The celibate must equally be chaste in mind. This means that he or she must foster chaste thoughts. The ninth commandment forbids us to have lustful thoughts: "You shall not covet your neighbor's wife."

Our Lord, in the Sermon on the Mount, reinforces this teaching when He says:

> You have heard that it was said, "You shall not commit adultery." But I say to you that every one who looks at a woman lustfully has already committed adultery with her in his heart. If your right eye causes you to sin, pluck it out and throw it away; it is better that you lose one of your members than that your whole body be thrown into hell. And if your right hand causes you to sin, cut it off and throw it away; it

is better that you lose one of your members than that your
whole body go into hell. (Matt 5:27-30)

The virtue of chastity and its opposite, the vice of
impurity, begin in our thoughts. What we think moves into our
hearts and forms our desires. The celibate person must therefore
be chaste also in desire. Our Lord tells us that if we deliberately
desire knowingly and freely lustful feelings or actions, these very
desires become the equivalent of the action itself. In our day and
age, with its widespread pornography, it has become increasingly
important for celibate persons to guard both their thoughts and
desires, so as to avoid powerful inner temptations.

Chastity in the mind also involves the mind's two
secondary powers, the imagination and the memory. Both of
these can cause disturbances and temptations against chastity.
The imagination, like a TV screen, presents images or mental
pictures of sexual stimuli that arouse strong passionate feelings
and desires. The memory, drawing from stimuli received in the
past, can produce similar effects. The memory can recall sexual
stimuli from past willful experiences as well as from unwilled
experiences as in the case of rape or sexual child abuse. In these
instances, the imagination and memory must be countered by
both prayer and self-discipline.[3] As a person makes progress in
the practice of the virtue of chastity, they will usually experience
a gradual lessening of passion, longer periods of peace, and
greater self-control. This is only a general effect, however, since
the person will undoubtedly still experience longer or shorter
periods of intense sexual passion. But if the growth in chastity
of mind is genuine, there will be noticeable times of calm and
freedom from sexual temptations.

CHASTE IN HEART

Finally, celibate persons must be chaste in their hearts.
This is because celibacy, which involves the renunciation of

marriage, also involves the surrender of those affections proper to husband and wife. Every person has the right to marry.

Celibate persons, for the sake of the kingdom of heaven, renounce this right. Since they still retain their human affections, however, they must continue to guard their hearts so they do not fall romantically in love with someone, thereby endangering their commitment to possess an "undivided heart."

Celibate persons must discipline their affections in order to remain focused on Christ. This does not mean that they do not love; Christ commands all His followers to love others as He did. What it does mean is that the celibate person must not allow the affections of his or her heart to focus on one person in an exclusive and possessive manner. Rather, there must be a certain loving openness to all, embracing all for the sake of Christ. Jesus must be at the center- of the celibate person's heart because his or her consecration focuses on Christ. From this love for Christ, the celibate's love flows out freely and generously to others. Someone once said that the danger for a celibate person is not in loving too much, but in loving too little, that is, letting his or her love focus on just one person rather than being free and open to focus on all as far as possible.

Celibacy therefore is really a "stimulus to love" because celibate persons must renew their consecration every day, making those free choices that will safeguard their celibate commitment. This requires that such persons be motivated by a true love for the Lord. In the face of the temptations that celibate persons experience, sometimes on a daily basis, such love will be strengthened, deepened and purified.

EXAMPLES OF THE SAINTS

None of us knows how intense our personal struggles will be or how long they will last. Even for some of the saints, the challenge of celibacy was by no means easy. It is said that, for a time, the youthful St. Benedict of Nursia, the father of Western monasticism, experienced severe temptations against chastity, and he almost succumbed to them. Overcoming them finally, after a long, bitter struggle, he was freed from such temptations in the latter part of his life.

St. Francis of Assisi also endured frequent and severe trials regarding chastity. His confessor, one of the priest-friars called Brother Leo, once saw St. Francis in a vision climbing the mountain of chastity. St. Francis reached the top of the mountain only after the greatest struggle. St. Francis would often go to extremes to overcome temptations. There were times when he would throw himself into the snow or into thorn bushes to break the temptations that afflicted him. He also mortified himself, fasting severely and allowing himself little sleep. All this he did, motivated by great love, so that he might remain faithful to Christ.

St. Catherine of Siena, too, experienced strong temptations against chastity. One time, a particularly violent and prolonged struggle lasted over a period of two days. When the temptations finally ended, our Lord appeared to her. St. Catherine asked Him: "Lord, where were you when I needed you during this trial?" Our Lord answered her: "Catherine, I was in your heart all along strengthening you!"

St. Alphonsus Liguori is known for his struggles throughout his life, even into his old age. The story is told that one time when he was about eighty years of age, a woman came to see him. He told her to sit on one side of the desk, and he would sit on the other. He said to her, "I have blood in my veins, not water!" He certainly struggled to remain faithful!

FAITHFUL TO THE END

A humorous story is told about an old priest (about seventy-five years of age) and a young, newly ordained priest. The young priest asked the elderly priest, "Father, are the temptations over at seventy-five?" "Oh yes," came the reply.

"They are over at seventy-five!" The next day the elderly priest saw the young priest and said to him "Father, make that seventy-six!"

Persons committed to celibacy do not lose or destroy their human nature with its many attractions and desires. Rather, they must deal with their sexual desires, whether they spring from physical or emotional feelings or from images of the senses or from the affections of the heart. The Holy Spirit, through the fruit of chastity, provides the necessary self-discipline to keep those desires always under control.

The long history of the Church and the experience of many individuals bear witness to the fact that the continuous renunciation of sexual pleasures and satisfactions, out of love for the Lord, becomes a unique way of daily dying with Christ. Thus purified, celibate persons are left with a uniquely undivided heart with which to love and serve the Lord and His people.

Notes

1. This total renunciation of all directly sexual or genital actions is called the virtue of continence. Canon 599 of the Church's *Code of Canon Law* states:

> The evangelical counsel of chastity assumed for the sake of the kingdom of heaven as a sign of the future world and a source of more abundant fruitfulness in an undivided heart entails the obligation of perfect continence in celibacy.

2. For a good explanation of modesty, read paragraph numbers 2521 through 2524 in the *CCC*.

3. It is important to point out that no temptation against purity, no matter how intense or disturbing, ever equals a sin against purity, as long as such a thought or desire is not wanted or accepted. In spite of any attraction it might have for us, if we resist and do our best to withhold our consent, then not only

have we not committed a sin of impurity, but we have actually practiced the virtue of purity.

CHAPTER 5

A Gift Chosen in Freedom

The Catholic Church teaches that celibacy is a free gift. It is free on the part of God who bestows it on those whom He chooses, calling them, inviting them, but never forcing them. It is also free on the part of those who are called, because they can only respond to this call and choose this gift in freedom. The reason for this freedom is that celibacy is a counsel, not a commandment. If it were a commandment, it would be obligatory for all people. But as an evangelical counsel, it is an invitation to commit oneself totally to following Christ in the Gospel way of life.

The individual is always free to choose to accept the invitation to live according to the evangelical counsels or not. Freedom means there is a real choice, a real possibility of accepting "options" between two goods. If something obstructs or eliminates any possible option, then there is no real choice. For example, to say, "I have no choice but to be celibate. . ." would indicate a lack of freedom precisely because there is a lack of choice in the matter. The possibility of choice, on the other hand, safeguards freedom and, therefore, love. The individual must be able to say, "I freely choose to accept celibacy." The only true motive for the choice of celibacy is love, given in freedom. This means it cannot be forced or demanded. There is no more validity to a "shot-gun celibacy" than there is to a "shot-gun wedding"!

Furthermore, it is only when love is freely given that it has the best chance of survival. In times of trials, it is important for the celibate person to remind himself or herself: "I freely chose this." In turn, love that is not forced or coerced, but given freely, can only be sustained by constant fidelity. The Servant of God Pope John Paul II, in speaking to priests and religious about their vow of celibacy, said, "The God who heard you say, 'Yes,' does not now want to hear you say 'No.':

Let us look more closely now at the element of freedom in choosing celibacy as it is reflected in the teachings of Christ and of St. Paul.

OUR LORD TAUGHT
THE COUNSEL OF CELIBACY

The teaching of Christ on celibacy (Matt 19:10-12) emphasizes the need for freedom and generosity in choosing it. Recall the circumstances in which this teaching was given. It follows the declaration that divorce would not be permissible for those who followed Him. The apostles reacted to our Lord's prohibition against divorce by asking: "Then who should marry?" Our Lord then takes the opportunity to set forth His teaching on celibacy. He begins by stressing the point that celibacy is not for all to embrace: "Not all men can receive this saying, but only those to whom it is given" (Matt 19:11).

As mentioned above, celibacy is a counsel offered to some, not a command imposed on all. Our Lord's words indicate that a two-fold "grace"[1] must be given to the individual: the call itself, which comes from God, and the actual grace to accept that call. The call of God is always mysterious: "Why is one person called and not another? Why is one grace or gift offered to one individual and not to another?" The answer lies hidden in the mercy and wisdom of God and His plan. However, it can confidently be said that God arranges all things for the benefit of each individual as well as for the welfare of the whole Church. Ultimately, all that God arranges works for His greater honor and glory and for our sanctification.

Our Lord next presents a list of contrasting reasons why a person might not marry and therefore live as a celibate (Matt 19:12). The contrast is important because it highlights the essential ingredients of freedom and generous love necessary to respond to the call and gift of consecrated celibacy. For purposes of study, it will be helpful to examine the *Revised Standard Version*[2] (*RSV*) translation of our Lord's words:

> For there are eunuchs who have been so from birth, and there are eunuchs who have been made eunuchs by men, and there are eunuchs who have made themselves eunuchs for the sake of the kingdom of heaven. (Matt 19:12)

The *RSV* (and translations similar to it) follows the original Greek text of the New Testament very closely, almost literally.[3] The word "eunuch," which means a castrated male, is found in the original Greek version. As a result of castration, a eunuch was not capable of normal sexual relations. For this reason, eunuchs were usually in charge of the women's quarters in ancient Eastern households. For the same reason, they also often won the confidence of the king and obtained for themselves positions of power and trust, such as ministers of the court.[4]

It must be noted that the word eunuch, in the above text, is used in reference to all persons who do not engage in sexual relations, for whatever reason. Our Lord presents three contrasting reasons which can account for persons being eunuchs, and, consequently, celibates excluded from marriage. It is important to recognize that the first two causes are not voluntary; only the third cause is freely chosen.

Those Born Celibate

The first category of eunuchs are those who are incapable of sexual activity "from birth." This seems to refer to those born incapable of engaging in normal heterosexual relations. Such impotence can result from either physical problems (for example, the lack of or malformation of sexual organs) or from psychological disorders (for example, fear, anxiety, anger). True impotence means there is no physical or psychological possibility of normal sexual relationships This impossibility, in turn, destroys or at least blocks the attraction and desire for a sexual relationship in marriage. Now, if there is no attraction or desire, there can hardly be any real inner freedom of choice and consequently little or no generous love as a motive. This is obviously not what our Lord means by celibacy for the sake of the kingdom of heaven.

Those Made Celibate

The second category of eunuchs are those who are deliberately made incapable of sexual activity "by men." This primarily refers to those men who are physically castrated for one reason or another, as happened in ancient times. This was likely not a voluntary procedure! In spite of castration, however, many eunuchs probably still felt some sexual attraction or desire, but because of their condition they could not engage in normal marital relationships Again, this form of celibacy was not freely chosen, as our Lord stresses is necessary for being celibate for the sake of the kingdom of heaven.

This second category could be extended to include others whom society prevents from marriage, for example, vast numbers of slaves in our Lord's time. Unlike the first group of "eunuchs from birth," the slaves would well have had normal attraction to and desire for marriage, but they often did not have the freedom to marry. Being slaves, they could not choose for themselves a particular way of life, nor the kinds of activities they wanted to engage in. They were totally dependent on the consent of their masters. In this case, celibacy was imposed by society. As with those celibate from birth, this is not the kind of celibacy to which the Lord calls persons for the sake of the kingdom of heaven.

Those Choosing to be Celibate

Only the third category of eunuchs, those who "have made themselves eunuchs for the sake of the kingdom of heaven," freely choose celibacy out of the motive of love. In the first two categories, celibacy was the result of physical, psychological, or social conditions that were not freely chosen. In this third category, the cause of celibacy is spiritual; it involves the voluntary choice of one's free will aided by God's grace.

For Christ, the freedom to choose celibacy rests on the fact that it is done "for the sake of the kingdom of heaven." This means that the choice is made out of love for God and for His Church. This celibacy enables those who embrace it to follow Christ's example and teachings totally, without the cares and concerns that marriage and family life bring. These celibates are able to dedicate themselves more fully to the needs of the spiritually or materially disadvantaged, again, in the light of the Gospel and for the sake of the kingdom.

When our Lord speaks of this third category as making themselves eunuchs, He does not mean this in a physical way.[5] By "eunuchs," Christ here means individuals who freely choose to refrain from sexual activity for the sake of dedicating themselves more completely to God and to the Church. It would be by constant self-denial and self-control, motivated by love, that Jesus' disciples would become "eunuchs," renouncing sexual activity and embracing the celibate state.

Our Lord concludes His teaching on celibacy when He

says: "He who is able to receive this, let him receive it" (Matt 19:12).

What Christ is saying is that any person who feels the attraction to celibacy for the sake of the kingdom and is generous enough to accept it, should actually accept it. He stresses the quality of generosity. The person who embraces celibacy for the sake of the kingdom freely renounces something of great personal importance.

That is not the case with the first two forms of celibacy. In the case of those who are celibate "from birth" (impotent), there is usually no attraction toward marriage. Therefore, there is no renunciation of something desired. In the second form of celibacy, those who are made celibate "by men" (castrated or enslaved), there may be desire, but there is no freedom. But for those who choose celibacy "for the sake of kingdom of heaven," there should be some attraction to and desire for marriage (or at least some recognition of its dignity, beauty, and possible fulfillment).

This is important because only if one is free to choose marriage as an alternative "option" in life, is he or she free to renounce it or surrender it in order to choose celibacy in love as another "option." Freedom of choice, therefore, safeguards and perfects the motivation of love; love, in turn, provides the generosity necessary to choose. This is why our Lord concludes His teaching by saying that it is the one with the generosity to do so who should accept celibacy; this is a teaching that cannot be readily understood, much less embraced, by all.

In conclusion, the contrasts that Christ presents in His teaching on celibacy highlight the importance of freedom in embracing it. To give up marriage "for the sake of the kingdom of heaven," a person needs to have some attraction and desire for it on the one hand, and some freedom to accept it or renounce it on the other hand. These factors of desire and freedom help to ensure a sufficiently generous and free love which is necessary to make the life-long sacrifices involved in a celibate commitment.

ST. PAUL ENCOURAGES THE PRACTICE OF CELIBACY

Esteem for Virginity

The teaching of St. Paul on celibacy is found primarily in chapter seven of the First Letter to the Corinthians. Regarding virginity, St. Paul admits that he has no commandment from the Lord (again, it is a counsel); however, he gives his own opinion, which he calls "trustworthy." This opinion is that it seems to him better for persons not to marry, but if they do, they do not sin (cf. 1 Cor 7:25-28).

He also clearly prefers that his Corinthian readers be celibate as he himself was. However, he sets forth certain qualifications to his exhortation. He recognizes, for example, that not everyone receives the same gift from God some receive the vocation to married life while others receive the call to celibacy (cf. 1 Cor 7:7).

The Need for Self-Control

St. Paul recognizes another factor that can keep people from embracing celibacy, which is the lack of adequate self-control required to live it. On this point, he says that it would be "better to marry than to be on fire" (1 Cor 7:9).[6] The expression "to be on fire" seems to refer to uncontrollable sexual passion. A person lacking the necessary self-control will never find peace or joy in celibate living. In contrast, though there will be conflicts arising from this choice (perhaps for extended periods of time), for those who truly receive the gift of celibacy there will be peace, tranquillity, and joy; it is a gift and fruit of the Holy Spirit, Who ultimately brings joy and peace to those individuals in whom He dwells.

St. Paul's emphasis on the need for self-control is made in light of the fact that celibacy is most often embraced as a life-long commitment. Therefore, it can only be undertaken with the help of God's grace. It furthermore requires a necessary maturity in the practice of virtue to be able to endure its constant demands.

Our Lord says in the Gospel of Luke (cf. 14:28) that if a man were going to begin to build a tower, he should first sit down and figure out if he has enough money to complete the project. If he lacks the necessary resources it would be imprudent for him to even begin building. St. Paul observes that this same principle is true of all those choosing a life of celibacy. If they have not gained some basic self-control in the area of chastity, they should consider carefully whether they could or should undertake the serious obligations of celibacy. They might either delay their choice until they have grown stronger in the practice of chastity (with their sexual passions under control), or else consider that marriage is the vocation to which God may be calling them.

St. Paul also speaks of "temporary" periods of celibacy for married couples. He sees that such periods can be spiritually profitable, providing married persons with periods of solitude and prayer. He cautions that they should abstain from sexual relations only as long as they do not risk the danger of sin, due either to temptations inspired by the devil (who would want to stop their practice of prayer) or to inadequate self-control on the part of one or both parties.

Celibacy in Difficult Situations

It is interesting and important to note that St. Paul is writing about celibacy to the Christian community at Corinth in Greece. In ancient times, Corinth had such a bad reputation that the expression "to live like a Corinthian" meant to live an immoral life; a "Corinthian girl" usually referred to a prostitute. It was a seaport with many travelers coming and going; these travelers were catered to with an abundance of immoral practices. Probably even more significant was the presence of a temple dedicated to the Roman goddess of love, Aphrodite, whose cult seems to have involved widespread sacred prostitution. Yet, it was to this Corinthian community of Christians, living in such immoral surroundings, that St. Paul not only counseled fidelity in marriage but even encouraged celibacy. The gift of celibacy can be offered by the Lord and freely embraced by His followers even in the most morally difficult of times or circumstances.

The "Undivided Heart"

St. Paul placed such emphasis on celibacy—even encouraging his Corinthian readers to live celibately as he did—because he viewed the celibate man or woman as a person with an "undivided heart." He contrasts the married person as "divided," needing to please both the Lord and his or her spouse. The unmarried person, instead, is "undivided," free to focus upon the Lord. Celibacy allows those who embrace it to be more attentive to prayer and to works of charity.

In summary, it is evident that.St. Paul encourages celibacy over marriage. But he also emphasizes that this decision must always be made freely. He says that it is not wrong to marry, but he feels that people who marry will have trials in this life, and he wants to spare those who, have not yet embraced the married life from these trials (cf. 1 Cor 7:28). He goes on to say that he has no desire to place restrictions on the Corinthians as to whether they marry or not, but only desires to promote what he feels will be most beneficial to them. He simply wanted to help his Corinthian converts find a way to devote themselves more completely to the Lord (cf. 1 Cor 7:35).

Notes

1. "Grace" is from the Latin word *gratia*, meaning a free gift. We need God's grace or help to achieve any good in the spiritual life, for Our Lord tells us that without Him we can do nothing (cf. John 15:5). St. Paul says that God must work in us both to "will" (the grace to desire his gifts) and to "accomplish" (the grace to accept His gifts and put them into practice) (cf. Phil 2:13).

2. The *Douay-Rheims* translation, published by the Confraternity of Christian Doctrine, reads almost the same as the *RSV* in this instance.

3. The *New American Bible* gives what might be called an "interpretative translation." For example, for the third category of celibates, the translators stress the free choice of renouncing sexual activity for the sake of the kingdom of God. It reads:

> Some men are incapable of sexual activity from birth; some men have been deliberately made so; some there are who have freely renounced sex for the sake of God's reign. (Matt 19:12) (NAB)

4. An example of this was the Ethiopian eunuch of Queen Candace, who was converted and baptized by Philip, one of the first seven deacons. He was in charge of the Queen's entire treasury. (cf. Acts 8:27)

5. There have been, in the history of the Church, certain people who have taken the teaching of Our Lord in this third category in a literal, physical way. A classic example of this in Church history occurred around the early part of the third century. Origen was an outstanding Scripture scholar and the head of the Church's first catechetical school located at Alexandria in Egypt. Motivated by a very literal reading of the Gospel text, it seems that Origen castrated himself in order to follow Jesus' teaching. He obviously interpreted Jesus' statement about "eunuchs" in a literal, physical manner.

When Origen later left his native Alexandria and went up to Caesarea and Palestine to teach, he was ordained a priest. However, his bishop in Alexandria was so upset he had left Alexandria that he claimed Origen's ordination as a priest was invalid because, having castrated himself, he was no longer a "true man." This became a notorious case in the early Church. Obviously, Origen, in his great zeal, gave a literal interpretation to Our Lord's words that Our Lord Himself never meant.

6. The *Douay-Rheims* translation reads: "It is better to marry than to burn." "To burn" was traditionally thought to mean "to burn in hell." This might well be the case if a person, lacking perseverance in celibacy, falls into unrepented sexual sins and ends up losing his or her eternal salvation.

CHAPTER 6

Freedom Requires Proper Motivation

Freedom protects and fosters love. In fact, freedom is the only proper environment in which genuine Christian love can grow and be sustained. This is because freedom implies a choice, a "yes" or a "no." Making a vocational choice is like coming to a fork in the road. One road will be marked "marriage," the other "celibacy." If, for example, the road to marriage is blocked off, then the individual could not freely choose celibacy. The person would have to admit: "I have no choice!" The same would be true if the road to celibacy were blocked off and the road to marriage was the only one open.

GOOD MOTIVES

True freedom to choose depends on having the right motivation. A person's motives for choosing celibacy are extremely important. Such a choice must be based on a supernatural motive[1] because it implies a response to God's call. The primary motive should be the love of God.

A person may be attracted to celibacy as a means to

dedicate his or her life more completely to God or in order to focus more on prayer and other practices of the spiritual life. Another good motive for embracing celibacy is wanting to respond more fully to the needs and concerns of the Church. This can be in the form of an attraction to helping others especially the poor and the underprivileged with their spiritual and temporal needs. There are various ways to serve which celibates can embrace full-time because they are free of family or marital responsibilities.

Those who choose celibacy, especially if called to the priesthood or religious life, must also be ready to witness to Christ in a public way; Christ must clearly be first and foremost in their lives. Again, the "undivided heart" of the celibate provides a unique means for doing this.

MIXED MOTIVES

It must be recognized that those who embrace celibacy for basically good motives may also have certain less adequate motives that affect or influence their choice. We could call this a kind of mixed motivation.

For example, the Lord can attract young people to a celibate vocation because of their friendship with religious men or women, or with priests in their parish with whom they are friendly. These young people may know very little about the lifestyle of priests or religious, or even what celibacy implies. But the Lord often uses friendship, good example, or the works of service which priests and religious do to stir up a desire for a religious or priestly vocation in a young person.

The understanding of celibacy and what is needed to embrace it generously, wholeheartedly and perseveringly will hopefully become clearer as the young person begins to follow his or her vocational call.

MOTIVES IN SPECIAL CIRCUMSTANCES

God can call a person to celibacy through any number of circumstances—even some that seemed negative at first. As St. Paul reminds us, for those who love God, all things can work together for a good purpose (cf. Rom 8:28). In such situations, a person's decision to embrace consecrated celibacy should be more carefully examined. For example, celibacy can begin when married life ends, as when one's spouse dies. I have also known cases in which married couples voluntarily agreed to separate, and one or both partners petitioned the Holy See for permission to enter religious life or the priesthood,[2] and they received it. In these cases, God apparently inspired the call to celibacy even within the context of marriage.

In other situations, God's invitation to a celibate commitment may be discerned only when an apparent marriage ends and is declared null. (A person who is separated or divorced civilly but does not have a Church annulment is neither free to remarry nor to enter priesthood or religious life.[3]) It is important that an individual who has gone through the experience of a divorce and declaration of nullity of marriage not enter a seminary or a convent on a "rebound," saying in effect, "Since marriage did not work out, I guess I'll choose to become a priest or religious!" Such a sudden decision for vowed celibacy might well be made with only a minimum of inner freedom since the person's newly celibate situation was not freely chosen. If over the course of time the person sincerely feels called to make a vow of perpetual celibacy, there should be reasonable evidence and the conviction of there being a true call to it.[4]

INADEQUATE OR "WRONG" MOTIVES

Acceptance by Necessity

Of even greater concern are those motivations that could

be called inadequate or "wrong."

The playwright T.S. Eliott once wrote: "The last temptation is the greatest treason: to do the right deed for the wrong reason."[5] Certain motivations for choosing celibacy can be judged insufficient or even "wrong." Sometimes such reasons are unconscious; they are not perceived by the person making the choice for celibacy. An example of this would be young persons who enter religious life or the priesthood to please a parent. Parental expectation can be such a strong underlying motive for some young people that, in a desire to please one or both parents, they might choose a vocation obliging celibacy without really accepting celibacy in their hearts. Their main desire is not to live the life but to please their parents.

Inadequate or "wrong" motivations often lead to problematic reactions later in life. In the case of the above example, it may happen that a religious or priest leaves the celibate vocation and marries after the death of one or both parents. Often without realizing it, he or she had remained in the celibate life in order not to cause distress or disappointment to their parents. When the motivation ceases and the celibate person feels no other attraction to remain in the religious life or the priesthood, the decision is made to leave.

Another inadequate reason for embracing celibacy is simply that it is obligatory to religious life or, especially, to the priesthood. As a result, celibacy is accepted as a disciplinary matter rather than as a Gospel value and a way of committing one's whole self to the Lord and His people. With this attitude, celibacy is easily reduced to a "necessary evil" to be tolerated. A person who accepts celibacy only because he or she must in order to be ordained or professed does himself or herself a great disservice.

This "acceptance by necessity" inevitably leaves the person frustrated in the face of his or her psycho-sexual needs and desires. Without deeper motivation, celibacy can easily become a source of deep anger or resentment against Church authority and regulations. A cynicism that shows itself in coldness and hardness toward others—especially in ministry, but also in community living—is often the result. Such persons lack the adequate supernatural motivation needed to live their celibate life in peace, joy and loving freedom. They might well be tempted to violate their vows or promises, falling into scandalous behavior and ultimately leaving the priesthood or religious life. They need to seek deeper reasons for their celibacy so as to be able to deal appropriately with their psycho-sexual needs while freely serving the Lord and His people.

Fear of Sex

Among other inadequate or "wrong" motivations for choosing celibacy is the situation of those who have a fear of sexual activity. Perhaps more common in times past, it stems from an understanding of sex as something "evil" or as something to be avoided at all costs. This attitude can be instilled in young people by well-meaning but overly protective parents, who either never spoke about sex or did so only in negative terms.

Two other possible sources for a fear of sex are probably more likely. One of them is the experience of sexual abuse as a child. Sexual experiences forced upon a child form a distorted notion of sex which can remain ingrained for years. One result of sexual abuse as a child can be a tremendous fear of sex, causing the individual to avoid any possibility of sexual involvement as an adult. A person who fears or dreads sexual activity as evil could unconsciously reject marriage and choose religious life or the priesthood because it requires celibacy. In this way, he or she would simply not have to deal with the question of physical, sexual involvement.

This fear can and should be resolved so as to allow for the inner freedom needed to make a psychologically sound and peace-filled choice. Spiritual directors and directors in formation programs can help young people to deal with the experience of sexual abuse so that celibacy is not chosen as a reaction to fear. The candidate to priesthood or religious life must come to understand sexuality as a God-given gift, something that is fundamentally good.

It is important that those who have been sexually abused work through their fears while still in the process of making a choice for the priesthood or religious life. If the fear remains unresolved, a later emotional crisis may occur. In other words, from the extreme of fearing sex, the person may begin to experience first a lessening of the fear and then the realization that sex is not bad or evil as they had previously thought. This, in turn, could cause the opposite reaction of desiring sex very strongly, much like a pendulum swinging from one extreme to the other. This explains why some religious and priests, who at one time were quite embarrassed or fearful of anything to do with sexuality, become inappropriately involved sexually or suddenly leave their celibate commitment and marry.

There is a further need for those who have been sexually abused to work through feelings of anger toward the abuser. Unresolved anger can make living a celibate life even more difficult than it is because unresolved anger tends to make people cold, aloof, and harsh in their dealings with others. Instead, when chosen freely and with generous love, the true gift of celibacy, tends to make people warm, concerned, and kind toward others. With appropriate counseling and sound spiritual direction, anger which stems from past abuse can be resolved (or at least sufficiently diminished), and the person will come to possess the inner freedom needed to live the celibate life with a certain degree of joy and peace.

A second source for fear of sex involves those who freely engaged in sexual activity as teenagers or young adults. They may experience so much guilt or shame that they end up with a fear of or at least a very negative attitude toward sex as being something "evil." Like those sexually abused as children, these persons must be helped to work out their negative attitude or perception of sex so that, in accepting celibacy, they do not reject marriage as evil (since it involves sexual activity) or take on celibacy as a self-imposed "punishment." Those who freely vow or commit themselves to celibacy do not give something evil to God; rather, they surrender, as already seen, the possibility of a very happy married life. This surrender of something good would be very difficult for those who see marriage or sex as evil.

Another cause for fearing sexual involvement can be the experience of growing up in an unhappy home environment. Seeing their parents constantly arguing or fighting, perhaps separated or divorced, may have left the impression that married life is not at all attractive. Approaching the question of vocation later in life, they may come to that "fork in the road" and, in their minds, think that the road to marriage is blocked off. They might then choose the path to celibacy, feeling they had "no other choice to make."

Persons from this type of background must, come to recognize that, if they are going to surrender marriage, they must do so from a viewpoint that allows them to give up something basically good. This requires healing of anger and of negative feelings about the past, perhaps directed toward parents or brothers and sisters, or whoever might have been the source of unhappiness in the home. A great deal of forgiveness will probably be needed in this process. In the final analysis, it is important that the individual freely surrenders to God something that is understood as at least potentially good. This positive attitude supports, in a helpful and healthy manner, the choice in freedom to serve the Lord in a celibate life.

Escape from the world

Another inadequate or "wrong" motive for choosing celibacy is what can be called a "flight from a corrupt world" decision. Hamlet, in Shakespeare's drama, says to Ophelia: "Get thee to a nunnery." The world can be cruel and immoral, and we can properly desire to avoid its evil influence. But such a desire should not be the determining factor in choosing a celibate life as a priest or religious. We must be careful that we are not simply running from something; rather, we must choose to move toward something, or better yet, toward "Someone." It would be just as unacceptable for one person to choose celibacy as an escape from the moral. evils of the world as it would be for another to marry just to "get out of the house." Celibacy must be the result of a positive choice, not a negative reaction! Celibacy involves an invitation from the Lord; ours must be a free response.

Celibates committed to the kingdom of heaven must also have a sense of hope for the world. Especially those in the priesthood or religious life must often reach out in some form of ministry to help people who are caught in the evils of the world or who have been victimized or oppressed. This requires a sense of hope which sees that Christ has won the victory in all things by His death and Resurrection. Even in what appear to be difficult and "hopeless" circumstances, it is still possible for the Gospel to take root and bear fruit for the kingdom of heaven. An attitude of fleeing from a corrupt world in order to avoid dealing with it is contrary to the important aspect of service in the celibate commitment. Even those who enter a cloister or a monastery must still focus much of their hidden life of prayer and sacrifice on the spiritual and temporal needs of those in the world.

Fear of Responsibility

A third general category of inadequate or "wrong" reasons for choosing celibacy is a fear of responsibility. This can take many forms. For example, a person may have feelings of inadequacy about raising children and therefore wants nothing to do with them. This is an inadequate reason because it is not grounded in faith or in love of God or others.

Another fear of responsibility would be the fear or

unwillingness to serve. In regard to marriage, this might be expressed as an unwillingness to support one's spouse or children, or an unwillingness to serve as a homemaker or be a provider for or protector of children. Such fear of responsibility would in no way be an authentic Christian motive to embrace either marriage or celibacy, because both gifts from God demand the willingness to serve.

A final form of fear of responsibility is the unwillingness to surrender one's "personal freedom." Celibacy differs from those forms of bachelorhood chosen for self-centered purposes. One who lacks the generosity required to serve others as Christ served cannot genuinely choose celibacy for the sake of the Lord and His kingdom.

To enter the priesthood or religious life in order to escape responsibility is going from the proverbial "frying pan into the fire." Both priests and religious have a tremendous responsibility to the Lord and to His people. Our Lord says in the Gospel that to whom more is given, more is expected (Luke 12:48). Because priests and religious receive generous blessings from the Lord, they have greater responsibilities.

An example of this point is found in a story involving the famous Capuchin-Franciscan stigmatic priest, St. Pio (aka, Padre Pio). A man went to him and shared his desire to become a priest. Padre Pio discouraged him and told him to marry. Padre Pio told him, "It is better that you be a good father of a family than a bad priest." Padre Pio must have foreseen that this man would not take his responsibilities as a priest seriously, and that he could end up being a source of disedification and perhaps of scandal to others and of discredit to the priesthood—and perhaps even endanger his own salvation.

Seeking Security

A fourth inadequate or "wrong" reason to choose celibacy is to seek security in the religious life or the priesthood.

This security might be having one's "bed and board"

provided. This can happen in especially difficult financial times or in particularly poor areas of the world. Judging from past experience, seminaries are more often filled during times of financial depression than when economic times are good. In times of war, some people consciously or unconsciously entered seminaries to avoid the military draft.

Apart from these exceptional circumstances, very passive-type persons may seek security in the religious life or the priesthood. This includes those who feel they would not succeed in other vocations which appear to demand more personal maturity and independence. This would certainly be an inadequate motive because consecrated celibates soon come to realize that their whole security rests not in their circumstances but in the Lord to whom they commit their lives. This is very important. One who only seeks personal security might end up, as one speaker on religious life put it, "nesting." This means they could feather their own little nest and provide for themselves with not the least concern for others. Such an attitude is certainly contrary to the values of the Gospel and, therefore. to evangelical celibacy.

CORRECTING WRONG MOTIVES

It is important to point out that if a person has chosen to pursue celibacy for obviously "wrong" or seriously inadequate motives, he or she must redefine their motivation before making any final commitment, or even before taking initial steps in that direction. Good spiritual direction and perhaps some sound counseling can help to correct or readjust one's motivation.

Situations involving less than adequate reasons for choosing celibacy can be worked out even while a person is in a formation program, especially if there is evidence or promise that adequate reasons are emerging. Self-honesty, sincerity with one's spiritual director, confessor and counselor, earnest prayer and frequenting the sacraments are all essential ingredients in the process of clarifying one's vocational motivation.

It is extremely important that a seminarian or a person in a religious formation program who experiences serious doubts or problems concerning celibacy, or who questions their motivation for choosing it, should not continue on the road to ordination or final profession until the difficulties are adequately resolved. It might be prudent to take some "time off" to reconsider or clarify the reasons for desiring celibacy. Some time away should provide the opportunity and freedom to reevaluate whether one is adequately prepared to embrace the responsibility of living celibately in a peace-filled and joy-filled manner. It seems only reasonable that such disturbing doubts and fears should be sufficiently resolved, at least as far as God's grace and human weakness would permit, before a person is ordained or makes a vow of life-long celibacy.[6]

This is not the same thing as saying that all fear or hesitation is gone at the time of profession or ordination. This would not be in accord with human nature! Rather, since trust is the opposite of fear and clarity the opposite of doubt, it seems that a mature decision for life-long celibacy requires a growing confidence and assurance of being able, with the daily help of God's grace, especially the guidance and strength of the Holy Spirit, to fulfill the commitment undertaken. This confident assurance is based on God's loving goodness, mercy, and faithfulness. St. Paul reflects this confidence when he tells us that God, who has begun His good work in us (i.e., living His gift of celibacy), is faithful, and He will bring His gift and purpose in giving it to completion (cf. Phil 1:6).

SHOULD A PERSON WITH INADEQUATE MOTIVATION LEAVE?

A final area to be considered is the situation of those who have been ordained or have made perpetual vows of celibacy and only afterward come to realize that their reasons for embracing the celibate vocation were inadequate or wrong. The question arises: Should they leave? The Church has permitted some persons consecrated to celibacy to be dispensed from their commitment. This has especially occurred in situations where there was evidence of serious difficulties from the beginning, and the individual had been wrongly encouraged to continue, with no concern for personal readiness.[7]

However, someone already in the priesthood or religious life would do well to heed the advice given by St. Augustine.

He was once asked if a man, who had already been ordained a priest, were later to realize that he had no inner priestly call or vocation should leave the priesthood? Augustine answered to the effect that, "No, he should not leave; rather, he should pray to God to receive the inner vocation."

In other words, a person already in a final commitment to celibacy might someday be struck by the fact that they seem to have embraced this vocation for the wrong reasons. St. Augustine believes that such individuals owe it to themselves as well as to the Lord and to the people of God whom they serve to give serious consideration as to whether or not they can recommit to celibacy, but this time for good and proper reasons. Many people in this situation have given years of service. It seems unreasonable, even unthinkable, that the Lord would now turn away from a sincere desire on their part to recommit themselves for good reasons to His love and service.

The example of St. Thomas Becket (d. 1170) comes to mind. He was appointed archbishop of Canterbury at the age of 44 by King Henry II, who was his close friend. King Henry thought this move would give him control over both the Church and the State in England. However, once Thomas became a bishop, he realized that he now owed his allegiance to the Lord. Though he had been ordained for wrong reasons, he changed his heart and ended up serving the Lord for right reasons. He had been a worldly and ambitious man but, in his own words, he went "from a follower of hounds to a shepherd of souls." He was martyred at the hands of four men in the service of King Henry. As he fell dying, he uttered the words, "I accept death for the name of Jesus and in defense of the Church." Nothing is impossible to God's grace, and certainly grace would not be wanting to those who ask God earnestly for the gift of loving and serving Him faithfully.

Notes

1. We can distinguish between supernatural and natural motives: A supernatural motive is based on our faith in God. Examples of supernatural motives include doing something for the love of God, for our sanctification, for the eternal salvation of those for whom Jesus died on the cross. A natural motive is one based on purely human or worldly values and goals. It has no reference to our relationship to God or to eternal life. Examples of natural motives include doing things to seek popularity, educational opportunities, security, and the like.

2. St. Francis, in his Rule of 1223 AD, made provision for such situations.

The Code of Canon Law: A Text and Commentary (ed. Coriden, Green & Heintschel, Paulist Press, 1985), referring to Canon n. 1042, explains:

> The impediment [marriage] binds as long as the marriage bond exists. Therefore, it does not bind widowers or those who have obtained an annulment. In some cases the Holy See will dispense from this impediment if the wife consents, seeks admission to a religious institute, or at least gives assurance she will not interfere with her husband's priestly vocation (p. 731).

3. Since marriage is listed in canon law as an "impediment" or obstacle to entrance into a religious community (Canon 643, n. 2), a legal separation or a civil divorce from one's partner would not suffice to enter religious life. A person would have to petition the Holy See for a dispensation from this impediment. Generally, a civil divorce would be needed in order to finalize any financial matters or to prevent the partner from later trying to force the marriage back together again. Marriage is also an "impediment" to ordination as a priest (Canon 1042,n. 1). However, the Holy See can dispense from this impediment if the wife consents, and either seeks admission to a religious community herself, or promises she will not interfere with her husband's priestly vocation.

4. The following example illustrates the point that the call to celibacy must be examined in context: Archbishop Sheen once said that during a retreat he preached for priests, he converted two men who were communists. They had become priests for the sole purpose of causing scandal and disruption inside the Church so as to try ultimately to destroy it from within. They entered the priesthood with the worst possible motivation, but ended up being converted and remaining as priests with the best of motivations!

5. "Murder in the Cathedral," T.S. Eliott, *T.S. Eliott: The Complete Poems and Prays* (Harcourt, Brace & World, Inc., New York, 1971), p. 196.

6. The document of Vatican II on religious life, *Perfectae Caritatis*, addresses this situation clearly:

> The observance of perfect continence touches intimately the deeper inclinations of human nature. For this reason, candidates ought not to go forward nor should they be admitted to the profession of chastity except after really adequate testing and unless they are sufficiently mature, psychologically and affectively. Not only should they be warned against the dangers

to chastity which they may encounter, they should be taught to see that the celibacy they have dedicated to God is beneficial to their whole personality (n. 12).

7. In this situation, the Church is following a practice similar to her granting of annulments in marriages. An annulment is a declaration that something essential was missing from the very beginning of the marriage. As a result, the Church judges that there could not have been a true internal consent of both partners to the marriage from the beginning. This is why the Church declares such a marriage "null."

CHAPTER 7

Why Make
a Vow of Celibacy?

Some years ago, I baptized a baby in a parish in New Jersey. After the ceremony, I was invited to the family's house for refreshments. As I was sitting in the living room with the other guests, a young boy walked into the room. He spotted me with my Franciscan habit, cord, rosary beads, sandals, and beard, and must have wondered not only who I was, but what I was.

He came and sat down right next to me. Feeling not a bit self-conscious, he began to talk to me about a number of different things.. All of a sudden, he spotted the three knots on my Franciscan cord (which stand for the three religious vows of poverty, chastity and obedience) and asked me in a whisper: "What are those knots?"

I didn't think he would know what a "vow" was, so I told him that I had made "three very special promises" to God, and each one of the knots represented one of those promises.

His eyes grew wide open when he heard this, but he soon began to talk again in a normal tone of voice about other things.

I forgot his question about the knots, but eventually he brought the conversation back to them again. In a secretive tone of voice, he asked me: "How do you make those knots?"

I decided to take one apart and remake it so he could see how it was done. As I began to untie the first knot, the little boy pointed at me and excitedly yelled: "Look at him! He's going to break his promise to God!" Needless to say, I told everyone that I was not really breaking my promise to God!

However, the little boy's response impressed me; even at such a young age, most people realize that promises should always be kept, especially promises made to God.

VOWS IN JUDAEO-CHRISTIAN HISTORY

Vows in the Old Testament

People have always made vows to God. We have evidence of this from the Bible, beginning in the Old Testament. For the ancient Israelites, the taking of vows ordinarily consisted of a promise to offer a sacrifice. These sacrifices were known either as a "free-will offering" or a "votive offering." By their very nature, free-will offerings and votive offerings were not commanded; they had to be offered and carried out spontaneously. (In fact, anything that was already commanded by law could not be the object of a vow or free-will offering.) The vows of the ancient Israelites always had to do with worship; vows to do works of charity for one's neighbor are not mentioned in the Bible.

All the vows spoken of in the Bible were taken by people in difficult situations. They needed God's special help, for example, to obtain victory over an enemy or deliverance from a plague. To be certain of obtaining God's special help in their need, they vowed that if He would come to their aid they would do a certain thing or omit doing something else. This gave rise to both "positive vows" and "negative vows."

In the case of "positive vows," if God answered the

petition of the person who made the vow, he or she would sing the praises of God in sincere thanks for the help or deliverance received. In thanksgiving for God's favor, something or someone is vowed to God or to His sanctuary. In the case of the Old Testament judge Jephthah, he vowed to sacrifice to God "whatever" would come first out of his household when he returned from battle if the Lord would give him victory over the Ammonites (cf. Jg 11:34-40).

A "negative vow" was a vow to abstain from something, such as fasting from food. Frequently, "negative vows" were strengthened or fortified by the taking of an oath. This meant that the person making the vow would lay a curse on himself if the vow was broken.

In later Old Testament times, certain abuses began to creep in, such as making too frequent and rash vows. The result was that many of these vows were neglected and never fulfilled. The abuse became so widespread that the religious significance of vows was diminished and the taking of vows was eventually discouraged. In some instances, where the actual vow could not be fulfilled, later Jewish legislation allowed the payment of the estimated value of the thing to be sacrificed to be offered in place of the thing itself. Still later, a prayer was introduced into the Jewish ritual for the Day of Atonement asking God to absolve all those vows which could not be kept.

Vows in the New Testament

In the New Testament, Our Lord cautions against abuses connected with certain vows but does not abolish vow-taking as such. In fact, we have evidence in the Acts of the Apostles that St. Paul made vows (cf. Acts 18:18; also see Acts 21:23).

Vows in Church History

In the early Church, men and women did embrace celibacy; however there is no indication that they took public vows of celibacy before the third century. St. Cyprian (d. 252 AD) considered virginity a permanent state from which a person might be released only by the bishop. If released, the person was then permitted to marry.

The first indication of public vows is found among the Eastern monks. From the time of St. Basil the Great (d. 379 AD), monks were committed to remain in their monasteries by a vow of stability. The monk vowed "a life," which seems to have embraced celibacy first of all, and secondly, the monastic life according to the particular rule the monk observed.

In the Western Church, the monks were also "vowed to the religious life." We have already seen how St. Benedict, the Father of Western Monasticism, had three vows for his monks, namely, stability, obedience, and conversion of life. We also indicated how poverty and chastity were implied in those vows. The first religious known to profess chastity explicitly, along with poverty and obedience were the hermits of St. Augustine (twelfth century). Pope Innocent III, at the beginning of the thirteenth century, spoke of chastity, poverty, and obedience as "essential to the monastic life." From that time on, poverty, chastity and obedience became the standard vows of all men and women religious.

WHAT IS A VOW?

It is important to see how a "vow" is understood in the Church today. Canon Law gives the following definition:

> A vow is a deliberate and free promise made to God concerning a possible and better good which must be fulfilled by reason of the virtue of religion. (Canon 1191, n. 1)

Let us look briefly at some of the elements of this definition. First of all, a vow is described as a "promise." By promise we do not mean a simple resolution like a New Year's resolution; nor is it even a more serious, firm resolution such as a person makes after going to Confession. The common understanding of the promise of a vow is that it is something we intend to keep out of a sense of obligation. Therefore, the promise of a vow involves the binding of one's self under the penalty of sin if broken.

The promise of a vow must be "deliberate." This requires two things on the part of the person who makes the vow. First, it requires the necessary intellectual ability to understand the seriousness of what one is doing when he or she undertakes the obligation of a vow. This assures that the person has the necessary maturity to make the vow.

The second quality needed to make a "deliberate" promise is that such persons clearly know what they are promising. If they were lacking essential knowledge of what they were going to vow or were in serious error about it, their vow would be invalid (non-binding). A person cannot properly give to God by a vow what they do not clearly understand.

Furthermore, the promise of a vow must be "free." This means that it must be made with unhindered freedom of choice. If a serious ("grave") and unjust force or fear were put upon someone so that the vow was made due to that fear, the vow would be invalid. This is true only if such force or fear is imposed unjustly by other people. On the other hand, normal fear or anxiety arising from within the person would not make the vow invalid, since a certain degree of fear is natural and is not unjustly imposed by others.

A vow is said to be "made to God." This is because a vow is an act of *latria*, that is, the worship and adoration given to God alone. For this reason, we cannot make a vow to the Blessed Virgin Mary or to any of the saints or angels. We can, however, make simple promises to them. We can also make a vow to God in honor of the Blessed Mother or the saints.

The next part of the definition says that the good thing vowed to God must be "better" and "possible." By "better," we mean that whatever good thing is vowed to God must be better than its opposite. For example, I can make a vow to God that I will give a large donation to help feed poor people because giving alms to the poor is better than doing nothing to help them.

A vow must also be a "possible" good. A person cannot make a promise to God which he or she cannot possibly fulfill. For example, I cannot vow to give $50,000 to feed the poor if I have only $5,000 to my name. If, after making a vow, a person becomes physically or morally incapable of fulfilling it, then they would be released from the vow.

As mentioned already, vows are considered an act of *latria* (the worship and adoration given to God alone) since they express our recognition of God's supreme dominion over us. As such, vows fall under the virtue of religion, which governs all our obligations toward God. A vow creates a new obligation toward God. If we fulfill this obligation, the goodness and merit of the act increases because we are practicing the virtue of religion. On the other hand, if the vow is violated, the guilt and malice of what we do increases because we violate the virtue of religion.

"CELIBACY FOR THE KINGDOM" ASSUMES A VOW OR PROMISE

Many Catholics live exemplary lives in the world as single persons. They faithfully practice chastity in mind, body, and affections. However, they would still not, strictly speaking, be considered "celibates for the sake of the kingdom." The reason is that there is no clear intention or decision on their part to continue as celibate for the rest of their lives.

Celibacy is a voluntary and permanent state of being without a spouse. It differs from a situation of simply "being single." A single person may be unmarried because he or she simply never met the right person or never had the opportunity to marry. This can happen in the case of people who must care for elderly or sick parents. Such a responsibility may hinder them from ever meeting and dating possible future marriage partners, and could also prevent them from marrying even if they did meet the "right person!"

In such situations, the person has not so much chosen celibacy as they have been compelled to remain single—like someone being carried along by the current of a stream. In such circumstances, celibacy is usually not freely chosen.

Celibacy for the sake of the kingdom of heaven, instead, must be an intentional or deliberate choice. At some point celibacy must be directly willed and not simply the result of ongoing circumstances. In our Catholic understanding, a celibate is someone who is both unmarried and who, for a supernatural motive, intends to remain so. This is why celibacy is a permanent state.

THE VALUE OF A VOW OF CELIBACY

Making a vow or promise of celibacy helps to ground the practice of celibacy on clearer and deeper reasons and motives. This can have beneficial effects, both on a psychological and on a religious level.

Psychological Value of a Vow
Expresses a Person's Intention Clearly

As already seen, the celibate consecrates his or her singleness to God in an act of generous love. The vow expresses clearly the intent to remain permanently unmarried for the sake of the kingdom of heaven. Because every vow of celibacy, even a private one, is made to God in the presence of a person who accepts this vow on behalf of God and of the Church, every vow of celibacy has some public or external expression. This external expression helps the individual making the vow to clarify and strengthen their intention to remain celibate.

If the intention to remain celibate was merely internal, never expressed externally in the form of a vow or promise, the person could easily change their mind (their intent) as time goes on. The vow, then, acts like a "fixed peg," a definite point of reference, that helps the person remain clear about what they have determined to do.

Sustains Our Determination

Once a person has clearly expressed the intention to remain celibate by a vow, the vow in turn can then support his or her determination to be faithful to it and becomes a source of added strength for the will. The vow also helps a person remain stable and consistent in the face of daily ups and downs. This is important because everyone's will power tends to waver and wane as time goes on.

Individuals often experience constant changes in their determinations, due to variations in mood or circumstances. People who allow themselves to be governed by their moods often feel attracted to one thing at one moment and to something else the next. Moods are an unstable foundation upon which to build one's resolve to live a celibate life.

Changed circumstances may also weaken a person's resolve. Some individuals have an internal desire or resolve to remain celibate when they do not have a potential marriage partner; but if that circumstance changes and they meet an attractive potential marriage partner, their determination may fade. The value of a vow, therefore, is that it stabilizes the person's resolve at the level of their best and most generous impulses. The vow, in other words, can help the person remain steadfast in their resolve and faithful over a long period of time. Like a compass that always points in the right direction, the vow will always point the individual celibate in the direction of faithfulness to the commitment made.

The Religious Value of the Vow

Observing the Sixth and Ninth Commandments

There are two obligations that follow from a vow of chastity. The first is the free renunciation of marriage. This obligation is unique to those who embrace celibacy. The second obligation is to observe the sixth and ninth commandments.

Married couples are also obliged to observe these commandments. For example, the sixth commandment deals with chastity in action and deed. Married persons must be faithful to their spouses, avoiding the sin of adultery. Married persons are obliged to observe the Church's teaching against the use of artificial birth control. They must also observe the ninth commandment that obliges chastity in thought and desire. This means that married couples must refrain from unchaste thoughts and desires about sexual relationships with people other than their spouse.

However, married couples have the right to enjoy sexual relationships with one another. This is part of their married chastity. Married couples also have the right to desire sexual relations with one another and to rejoice within the limits of chastity in these relations.

Unmarried persons are obliged to practice a chastity that excludes all directly sexual actions, whether alone or with others, as well as all directly sexual desires and thoughts that arouse the sexual pleasure intended for married couples. From their vowed commitment, celibates can draw strength and willingness to faithfully observe the sixth and ninth commandments according to their state in life. Since they freely renounce even the legitimate sexual pleasures they could have had in marriage, even more so will they renounce any sinful sexual pleasures prohibited for everyone by the sixth and ninth commandments.

Increases the Merit of Virtue

The obligation of all Christians to practice the sixth and ninth commandments rests on the obligation to practice the virtue of chastity. When individuals practice the virtue of chastity in thought and action, according to their state in life, they gain merit from God.

Celibates, however, have a second obligation to observe the sixth and ninth commandments. It comes from their vow of chastity which, in turn, involves the practice of the virtue of religion. The virtue of religion governs all our obligations toward God.[1] A vow is an act of the virtue of religion because it recognizes God's supreme dominion over us. It involves a sense of worship of God since it expresses our complete dependence on Him; this is all part of the virtue of religion. Therefore, when celibates observe the demands of the sixth and ninth commandments, they receive an increase of merit for their virtuous actions, because they are actually practicing two virtues at the same time: the virtue of religion as well as the virtue of chastity.

We could sum this up by saying that the vow of celibacy increases the merit of chaste actions, thoughts, and desires because two virtues are practiced and two obligations are fulfilled simultaneously. The first obligation is the obligation of the commandments; in fulfilling the sixth and ninth commandments the virtue of chastity is practiced. The second is the obligation of the vow; in fulfilling the vow of celibacy, the virtue of religion is practiced.[2]

Frees from Hindrances in the Spiritual Life

Vatican Council II, in its dogmatic constitution *Lumen Gentium* (Ch. 6, n. 44), tells us that another reason for the vows of a religious is to free the person from those things that hinder or hold them back from loving God ardently and worshipping Him perfectly. In the First Letter of John we read that we have three spiritual enemies. They are the world (also called the "concupiscence of the eyes"), the flesh (or the "concupiscence of the flesh"), and the devil (or the "the pride of life") (cf. 1 John 2:16).

These three obstacles can hold one back from loving God because they can gain control over the heart of the person. For example, our Lord tells us that no man can serve two masters, namely, God and money. What this means is that we cannot sincerely and wholeheartedly seek spiritual growth and materialistic gain at the same time. These two goals are mutually exclusive; a person will either come to love one and hate the other or else become so dedicated to one that he or she will neglect the other (Matt 6:24).

An example of this is found in the incident of the rich young man (Matt 19:16-22) who asked our Lord what he must do to gain eternal life. Jesus, in answer, told him to keep the commandments. When the young man insisted that he had done this all through his life, he asked what more he could do.

Jesus told him that if his dedication would be complete, he should go and sell all that he had, give the proceeds to the poor so that he would have treasure in heaven, and then he could come and follow Him.

But the Gospel tells us that the rich young man walked away sad; having many possessions, he did not want to part with them. These possessions became an obstacle or hindrance to his following Jesus more closely. The vow of poverty is meant to free the religious from such an obstacle.

The same is true of the religious vow of obedience. A person can be hindered in following Jesus by pride and selfwill. In renouncing self-will by the vow of obedience, a religious can be freed from such hindrances and so be able to accomplish the will of God more faithfully.

The same principle applies to chastity. We have already seen in St. Paul's teaching on celibacy that he considered married persons to have a "divided heart," needing to focus on loving and serving both God and spouse. On the other hand, the unmarried person is free to focus on the things of the Lord.

By freeing the individual from those responsibilities of married and family life that could, at times, prove to be hindrances in a relationship to God, the vow of celibacy allows the person to concentrate more fully on pursuing the spiritual life.

Allows a More Total Consecration of One's Self to God

All Christians, no matter what their vocation in life, are obliged to observe the virtues (not the vows) of poverty, chastity, and obedience. By the virtue of poverty, we mean that all Christians must live in such a way that they do not make an idol of money, nor become consumed by the pursuit of material gain, nor become so attached to riches that they cannot share their goods with the poor and needy. They may possess and use money and material goods, but in such a way that they are always in control of their riches and not let their riches control them.

The same is true of the virtue of obedience. Every Christian must practice it by seeking to obey the will of God; however, not every Christian is obliged to submit to the obedience of a religious superior by means of a vow in order to accomplish God's will.

Finally, all Christians must be chaste according to their vocation in life; however, not every Christian is obliged to be celibate (i.e., to not marry).

The obligation to observe the virtues of poverty, chastity, and obedience is part and parcel of the Christian life because of our baptism. By the vows, religious (e.g., monks, nuns, friars, sisters, brothers, etc.) simply deepen the consecration begun in baptism and build upon it. By public vows, they oblige themselves to live not merely the virtues of poverty, chastity and obedience, as every Christian is obliged to do, but they also take on the further obligations that each vow entails. The vow of poverty entails the renunciation of all material goods. The vow of obedience would oblige a religious to obey his or her rule of life and community superiors. Finally, the vow of chastity would oblige a consecrated celibate to renounce marriage.

The vows allow religious, therefore, to consecrate themselves more completely to God. Furthermore, the Second Vatican Council points out that by a vow of celibacy or chastity (as well as the other vows), religious are drawn more completely into the apostolic work of the Church. They become "public persons" in the Church because of their public profession of the evangelical counsels.

As can be seen, the vow of celibacy has many advantages for those who embrace it in freedom and love. It not only provides psychological and religious benefits that enrich the living of celibacy, it also increases the celibate's merits through a fuller and more intense consecration to God and His people.

Notes

1. The virtue of religion fits under the larger category of the moral virtue of justice, by which we render to everyone (including God) what is their due.

2. It must be added, however, that if a celibate violates the vow of chastity by deliberate unchaste actions, thoughts or desires, two sins are committed, because two obligations and two virtues are violated. Violating the sixth and ninth commandments violates the virtue of chastity (a sin of "unchastity"). Violating the vow of celibacy violates the virtue of religion (a sin called "sacrilege"—the violation of a sacred person, place, or thing).

CHAPTER 8

Problem Areas
for Celibacy Today

Proverbs teach a lot of wisdom in a few words. As we approach some of the problem areas of celibacy, two proverbs come to mind.

One is: "Fools rush in where angels fear to tread." Celibates come to realize that they cannot take unnecessary chances or needlessly expose themselves to dangerous risks in regard to living out their celibate commitment. There are certain things they should exclude from their lives if they wish to live in true Christian peace and joy. It would be foolish to act otherwise.

The second proverb is: "An ounce of prevention is worth a pound of cure." Reasonable prudence, caution, and discernment can not only considerably lighten the burdens that celibacy imposes, but they can also reduce the potential for grief.

The wisdom of these proverbs certainly applies to our efforts to sincerely live celibacy for the sake of the kingdom of heaven.

There are certain matters related to human sexuality and

Catholic moral teaching that are potential "problem areas" for celibates today. These areas can only be touched upon briefly here since each of them would require a volume in itself if treated in full detail. This chapter and the following three will deal with some of these areas.

DISTORTION OF
CATHOLIC MORAL TEACHING

Celibacy has become more difficult today because of a certain confusion regarding the moral teaching of the Catholic Church. Thirty years ago, one could pick up any book on Catholic moral theology and find the traditional Church teaching. Today, however, we come across a number of opinions from various theologians and writers of moral theology that are at variance with traditional Catholic teaching. This is especially true in the area of sexual morality. This includes discussions of premarital sex (fornication), extramarital sex (adultery), masturbation, homosexuality, contraception, and even abortion.

Today, many forms of immoral activity are being justified by theologians, who use arguments based on what is popularly known as "situation ethics."[1] They argue that "as long as it is done with love and concern and not selfishly" or "if no one gets hurt," the action is morally justified. But it must be asked: Whatever happened to the moral teachings of the commandment "Thou shalt not commit adultery?" Or the teaching of our Lord that anyone who looks with lust upon a woman commits adultery with her in his heart (cf. Matt 5:28)?

Part of the confusion in Catholic moral theology began in the late 1960s when Pope Paul VI issued the encyclical *Humanae Vitae.* There was widespread public rejection of the papal teaching condemning artificial birth control. This was one of the first times that modern Catholic moral theologians openly expressed opinions different from the official teaching of the Church, and, in some instances, in defiance of it.

Furthermore, much good work had been done in the 1950s and early 1960s in the area of psychology and personal responsibility. It helped us to understand how certain subjective factors involved in a person's moral behavior could influence and sometimes even lessen personal moral responsibility. By the late 1960s, however, one began to read in some books of moral theology that not only were there personal or subjective factors that could diminish guilt in certain instances, but that the moral teachings themselves could change. As a result of such reasoning, an act like adultery was not a serious sin in every situation, but could be justified by certain circumstances or needs. There was a great deal of movement in moral theology away from "absolute principles" (which cannot change because they are from God) to "relative" and "situational" norms (which can change or be adapted in different cases). This led to a widespread breakdown in traditional Catholic moral teaching on a popular level, resulting in much confusion among many sincere people as to what is authentically Catholic moral teaching and what is not.

This problem is not really a new one in the Church. St. Paul, in the very first generation of Christians, began to experience the problem of distorted moral teachings. He attributed this to people deceiving themselves because they wanted to justify their immoral behavior. He wrote to the Christians at Corinth:

> Do you not know that the unrighteous will not inherit the kingdom of God? Do not be deceived; neither the immoral, nor idolaters, nor adulterers, nor sexual perverts, nor thieves, nor the greedy, nor drunkards, nor revilers, nor robbers will inherit the kingdom of God. Shun immorality. Every other sin which a man commits is outside the body; but the immoral man sins against his own body. Do you not know that your body is a temple of the Holy Spirit within you, which you have from God? You are not your own; you

were bought with a price. So glorify God in your body (1 Cor
6:9-10, 18-20).

It is easy for a person to deceive himself or herself in
this matter. If we want sexual pleasure badly enough, we can
rationalize or excuse anything, or at least minimize it.

Archbishop Sheen has two interesting comments that
apply here. One is: "If you don't live what you believe, you
will end up believing what you live." The other comment has
to do with heresy (which can apply to the distortion of moral
teachings as well). He said: "People do not become heretics
because of what they want to believe, but because of how they
want to live!"

Again, we turn to the teaching of St. Paul as he wrote
to his converts at Ephesus. They had once been pagans given
over to all kinds of immoral sexual behavior. St. Paul reminded
them:

> Put off your old nature which belongs to your former
> manner of life and is corrupt through deceitful lusts, and be
> renewed in the spirit of your minds (Eph 4:22-23).

St. Paul taught that we can easily be swayed by our
"deceitful lusts," or our lustful desires and illusions. Our sinful
desires are the result of unruly passions, such as lust and
concupiscence. These passions pull strongly at our heart and
demand satisfaction. This is when the illusions come into play.
We begin to rationalize and justify our behavior with. statements
like: "It's not so bad! God is merciful, He understands!"
"Everybody's doing it today! After all, the old morality is
outdated!" These illusions serve to justify our consent to sinful
desires. We have ended up deceiving ourselves.

The same can be said for those who search for priests
and moral theologians who will tell them what they want to
hear. They go "shopping around" to find someone who agrees
with them. Again, St. Paul experienced the same thing in his

day. He wrote to his disciple, Timothy:

> Preach the word, be urgent in season and out of season, convince, rebuke, and exhort, be unfailing in patience and in teaching. For the time is coming when people will not endure sound teaching, but, having itching ears, they will accumulate for themselves teachers to suit their own liking, and will turn away from listening to the truth and wander into myths (2 Tim 4:2-4).

This moral confusion poses difficulties for all Catholics, but it can pose special difficulty for celibates and those discerning a call to celibacy. It can leave them with the impression that celibacy excludes marriage but permits other forms of sexual relationships which they think can be justified "in certain circumstances."

Anyone wishing to embrace the way of celibacy, however, must be ready to follow authentic Catholic Church teaching, which excludes all forms of directly sexual behavior outside of marriage. This is because celibacy implies not only giving up the right to marry, but also obliges the practice of the virtue of continence (the avoidance of all directly sexual actions whether alone or with others).

THE DANGER OF PORNOGRAPHY

Another difficulty for celibacy today is the spirit of the age in which we live. The psychoanalyst Sigmund Freud, who was very popular up until the 1970s, found the basis for all personal problems in the desire for sex. Greatly influenced by Freud, ours has been called the "post-Freudian age;" sex has become the answer for everything. It is the age that has produced such ideas as the "*Playboy* philosophy," where sex is seen as nothing more than recreation. It is an age that has separated pleasure from responsibility in terms of sexual activity. As a result, there is widespread promiscuity in our society; sex is taken casually and fewer life-long commitments are being made. This is reflected in the high rates of divorce and remarriage even among Catholic couples.

Both as a cause and a result of this promiscuity, pornography abounds.[2] It is seen in contemporary plays and films as well as in a vast number of books and magazines that cater to the sexual interests of people. The influence of pornography is even being brought into the homes of good people by means of television. This has had an especially negative impact on impressionable young people. Add to this certain problems that are spin-offs of pornography, such as incest, sexual abuse, and homosexuality, and we see the extent of the problem today.

Pornography Depersonalizes

Pornography produces a serious negative influence that is often not properly recognized: Pornography depersonalizes human sexuality. "Sexuality," it should be remembered, is far more encompassing than "sex." Sexuality is our total makeup as either male or female, all that goes into our masculinity or femininity. Each person, considered holistically, is composed of three interconnected elements: the physical, the emotional and the spiritual.[3] All three of these elements together form our sexuality or, more precisely, our psycho-sexual makeup as persons. To express ourselves as complete persons, we must express ourselves in a combination of all three of our psychosexual components with the physical, emotional, and spiritual interacting. "Sex," on the other hand, is limited to the physical or genital level of expression.

Pornography's Effects on the Married

In order to understand how pornography depersonalizes human sexuality, let us look at its negative effects on a marriage. Marriage is a unique and exclusive sharing with one another in a life lived together, a caring about one another in all aspects of life. As sacred Scripture says, "The two shall become one flesh"

(Matt 19:5). In the Christian view of marriage, a husband and wife should love each other as complete persons. This means they give to and receive from one another their total love. This total, mutual love is expressed in all three elements of their personhood: physical, emotional, and spiritual.

In marriage, sexual or genital actions (the physical element, including sexual intercourse and all those actions which lead up to it) are meant to be for husband and wife a sign and expression of their mutual love, self-giving, and openness to life. It is also a means of fostering this love and self-giving. To have the physical element (genital actions) without the emotional (caring) and the spiritual (loving and sharing) aspects is to destroy the unity, of human sexuality, reducing it to mere physical actions. This dehumanizes the psycho-sexual makeup, reducing the God-given sacredness of the human person to the merely biological level.

Sexual activity in marriage is a language of love between a husband and wife. Pornography, on the other hand, is never directed toward a person who is loved. It is "nameless" and therefore "personless" (i.e., depersonalized) sexual behavior. In pornography, there is no loving, no caring, no commitment. It is simply the using of the sexual attraction of others for lustful pleasure. The persons portrayed in pornography (for example, in movies or magazines) are always "objects."

Pornography comes from a Greek word that means the accounts of the deeds of prostitutes. As in prostitution, which is nameless and personless sex, the other person simply does not matter; he or she is there only for sexual gratification. He or she can be interchanged with other partners at other times or in other circumstances.

In contrast, the goal of Christian marriage is the establishment of a permanent state of mutual loving and sharing, in which husband and wife are the unique focus of this giving and receiving of love. This is a love which by its very nature can and must endure. It is also a mutual love than can never be substituted by or shared with any other persons. Furthermore, it is a love that should never be expressed in bodily action without the inner presence of the commitment of the heart! Pornography not only lacks these aspects, but is completely contrary to them. It is diametrically opposed to the Christian ideal of sexual love and to the God-given dignity of each human person.

Married couples who indulge in pornography usually experience, often without realizing it until it is too late, a gradual erosion of their marital love. Under the influence of pornography their marital intimacy becomes less and less a self-donation and more and more a using of one another for sexual gratification. When such disordered attitudes dominate a couple's thinking, they may begin to use artificial birth control (which limits their openness to one another as well as to life); this, in turn, often leads to forms of sexual behavior which focus on physical, genital pleasure, such as oral or anal sex. Because of the widespread influence of pornography, especially through television, these distortions of sexual behavior are becoming more accepted.

St. Paul refers to these distortions when he mentions that many of the ancient pagans, blinded by the practice of idolatry, became distorted in their sexual behavior, "to the dishonoring of their bodies among themselves" (Rom 1:24), and "for this reason God gave them up to dishonorable passions. Their women exchanged natural relations for unnatural. . ." (Rom 1:26).

These distortions of sexual behavior undermine true and respectful love of spouses for one another. In many cases where sexual behavior has become "nameless" and "personless," marital infidelity as well as divorce have followed. In some cases, it has led to grave moral disorders such as homosexuality and pedophilia (especially incestuous child abuse).[5]

Pornography's Effects on the Celibate

The effects of pornography on celibates are equally disastrous. Celibates must develop their sexuality as male or female, expressing their masculinity or femininity accordingly. But by their commitment, celibates do not express their sexuality on a physical level by sexual (genital) actions. They may, for example, express the common Christian signs of affection such as a simple kiss or hug with relatives, friends, colleagues, or persons whom they serve with in some form of ministry. The other aspects, emotional and spiritual, are the levels at which they principally communicate their loving, caring, and sharing with others.

If a celibate indulges in pornography, the first effect that usually occurs is to look upon other people as potential objects for sexual gratification. This is the "depersonalizing" of others. Another potential problem, masturbation, almost always follows. Pornography arouses passionate desires and genital feelings; acts of self-gratification are the almost inevitable outlet. Pornography can lead to further problems, such as fornication, adultery, or prostitution. Because much pornography today tends to be gravely disordered, homosexual relations may be sought. Finally, pornography can trigger such gravely pathological conditions as pedophilia (sexual child abuse) in persons with serious underlying sexual disorders.

Persons addicted to pornography are hardly capable of living chastely, much less of making a life-long commitment to celibacy. They must first mature both emotionally and spiritually. They grow emotionally by coming to realistically accept themselves and others. Addiction to pornography is often the result of significant narcissism, focusing oneself on personal gratification. Pornography may have its roots in immature adolescent-level behavior. Teenagers use pornography as a means of "acting out" inner tension and conflict. In order to break this narcissism and grow emotionally, a person must learn to genuinely care about others. He or she must break out of the narrow focus of self-centeredness.

Such persons must also grow spiritually; through prayer, self-denial, and charitable concern for others, especially the needy, one learns to discipline the sexual passions. This further breaks the enslaving chains of narcissism and allows at least the initial inner freedom to move out of self and toward God and others.

THE IMPORTANCE OF MODESTY

The practice of the virtue of modesty is essential to living celibately because it counters the addictive attraction of pornography. Modesty protects chastity by guarding against those sexual stimuli that come through the senses (especially seeing, hearing and touching) and that are potentially capable of stirring up lustful thoughts, desires, and feelings that could lead a person to commit sins of unchastity.

An example is modesty of the eyes. Our Lord speaks of the eye as the lamp of the body (Matt 6:22-23) which acts as an opening through which light is admitted to the soul. If the eye is healthy (good), the whole inner person is illumined with true light. If the eye is diseased (evil), the very source of light is darkened and the whole inner man is in total spiritual darkness.

What passes through our eyes? Human beings experience sexual arousal somewhat like the movements of the waves of the sea.[6] It varies in intensity and frequency with each person. When such arousal overcomes a person, it can be felt as restlessness, lustful curiosity, or prurient interest. It is a time to be more vigilant in guarding against temptation.

The experience of King David serves as a powerful example of the need for modesty of the eyes. The story is told in 2 Sam 11 of how King David, looking about curiously from the rooftop of his palace one evening, saw a beautiful woman,

Bathsheba, bathing. He lusted for her in his heart and ended up committing adultery with her. When she conceived a child from this sinful act, King David tried many devious means to cover over his sin, finally resorting to the murder of Bathsheba's husband, Uriah. God was greatly displeased with King David's sins. St. Jerome, using King David and also his son King Solomon as examples states: "Let us all take care we do not fall into sin, for none of us can hope to be as holy as King David or as wise as King Solomon!"

Jesus indirectly attacks a major consequence of pornography when He condemns deliberate lustful thoughts and desires in no uncertain terms

> You have heard that it was said, 'You shall not commit adultery.' But I say to you that every one who looks at a woman lustfully has already committed adultery with her in his heart (Matt 5:27-28).

Many world religions condemn the act of adultery as morally wrong. But only Jesus also condemns the voluntary thoughts and desires about those actions as being morally wrong. Evil begins in the heart; deliberate lustful thoughts and desires are the beginnings of the outward actions.

Our Lord stresses how important it is for His followers to resist such deliberate thoughts and desires. They must try to prevent them from unnecessarily coming into their minds and hearts or, when unavoidable, from consenting to them after they have come. Our Lord stresses that no matter what sacrifices we must make or struggles we must endure, we should do so willingly for the sake of winning eternal life:

> If your right eye causes you to sin, pluck it out and throw it away; it is better that you lose one of your members than that your whole body be thrown into hell (Matt 5:29).

Our Lord is never satisfied with mere external observance of God's laws, but rather He also requires an inner obedience.

He is not satisfied if one simply avoids hurting one's enemies; He wants us to love them. He is not satisfied with the avoidance of sinful acts like adultery; He requires a pure heart.

Two Helpful Points about Modesty

In practice, celibates should remember two important points. First, regarding modesty, a person must avoid more than what is absolutely sinful; in effect, he or she must avoid whatever can easily become sinful later on in moments of weakness.

Here, we can apply the proverb mentioned earlier: "An ounce of prevention is worth a pound of cure!" The media industry, for example, issues its own moral classifications for films, distinguishing between what it calls "hard core pornography" and "soft porn." They want to sell movies to the public, and so they want the largest potential audience. What may be "soft porn" (i.e., "not so offensive") by Hollywood's standards may actually lead Christians into grave temptations and sins.

Modesty does recognize a certain relative degree of application.[7] For example, a movie theme that might morally harm a child may not have any harmful effect on a mature adult. However, there are certain sexual stimuli that are so offensive that they will upset anyone and so must be avoided by everyone as unnecessary occasions of sin. There are other stimuli that, out of the virtue of prudence, should also be avoided. This is especially important for those committed to celibacy. These stimuli can easily return through one's memory and imagination to cause an otherwise avoidable temptation. This can result in at least a loss of inner peace, if not also a sinful fall into lustful thoughts, desires or actions.

Another point to consider is that pornography can easily become addictive and enslaving. St. Paul sets down a moral principle that can be helpful in guiding our practice of modesty; especially in regards to "borderline" material:

"All things are lawful for me," but not all things are helpful. "All things are lawful for me," but I will not be enslaved by anything. (1 Cor 6:12)

A second useful point to remember regarding modesty is that we cannot avoid all sexual stimuli. Pornography abounds in our society, and there is no way to avoid it completely. Our Lord Himself said that some scandal in a person's life is unavoidable (cf. Matt 18:7). St. Paul also recognized the fact that we cannot avoid all contact with people who promote immorality in the society around us "since then you would need to go out of the world" (1 Cor 5: 10).

Although we may not be able to avoid pornography completely, it can be said that if a person does not look for it, much of it will not come on its own. To control sexual curiosity is important; after all, curiosity can kill (and more than just cats!). When a person experiences a restless prurient interest, he or she may seek suggestive stimuli through various forms of media. It would not be surprising if, as a result of any suggestive material viewed, the celibate experiences severe lustful temptations and even falls into sins of unchastity such as masturbation. A person who is serious about his or her celibate commitment must establish clear and prudent norms to regulate the use of those media which often prove to be pornographic in content.

PORNOGRAPHY CAN INFLUENCE THE CALL TO CELIBACY

The widespread pornographic atmosphere in today's society can easily affect young people considering a choice of celibacy. It probably has already discouraged many of them from embracing celibacy by arousing constant allurements and causing severe struggles to remain chaste. It may have discouraged still others by promoting the false notion that if they are not sexually active they are missing the whole meaning of life.

On the other hand, for those who resist pornography's attraction and influence, one good effect can follow. It can motivate those who do choose celibacy in today's prevailing climate of immorality to do so with a deeper sense of dedication and commitment in their hearts. They will certainly have a very clear idea of what they are giving up!

Build on Rock, Not on Sand

In conclusion, if we sincerely wish to live our celibacy as Jesus both lived and taught it, we would do well to focus on the conclusion of the Sermon on the Mount:

> Every one, then, who hears these words of Mine and does them will be like a wise man who built his house upon the rock; and the rain fell, and the floods came, and the winds blew and beat upon that house, but it did not fall, because it had been founded on the rock. And every one who hears these words of Mine and does not do them will be like a foolish man who built his house upon the sand; and the rain fell, and the floods came, and the winds blew and beat against that house, and it fell; and great was the fall of it. (Matt 7:24-27)

Jesus' teaching is the only solid rock upon which to build our faith and, consequently, an authentic celibate life. He alone can give us the wisdom and strength to live celibacy in a loving, joyful, and peaceful manner, through His Holy Spirit, Who has been poured forth into our hearts (cf. Rom 5:5). Jesus' authentic teaching is found in the authentic teaching of the Catholic Church, which Christ established and to which He gave authority to teach in His Name. He says unconditionally: "He who hears you, hears Me" (Luke 10:16).

If we adhere to true Catholic teaching, we build on solid rock. When the trials and temptations, the storms of life come, we may be shaken, but we will ultimately survive. But to reject authentic Catholic Church teaching and to follow what deviates from it or even contradicts it is to allow ourselves to be deceived. We would be building on sand. We would lack an adequate support to withstand the storms of life. Our commitment to chaste celibacy would then, in our Lord's words, collapse and end in complete ruin!

Notes

1. For a good explanation of situation ethics and related topics, read the encyclical letter *Veritatis Splendor* by the Servant of God John Paul II. Available at www.papalencyclicals.net

2. The *CCC* defines pornography:

Pornography consists in removing real or simulated sexual acts from the intimacy of the partners in order to display them deliberately to third parties. It offends against chastity because it perverts the conjugal act, the intimate giving of spouses to each other. It does grave injury to the dignity of its participants (actors, vendors, the public), since each one becomes an object of base pleasure and illicit profit for others. It immerses all who are involved in the illusion of a fantasy world. It is a grave offense. Civil authorities should prevent the production and distribution of pornographic materials (n. 2354).

3. An ancient group of Greek philosophers called the Neoplatonists held that human beings were composed of body, soul, and spirit. Today, we generally speak of our physical, emotional, and spiritual makeup.

4. The *CCC* condemns prostitution with these words:

Prostitution does injury to the dignity of the person

who engages in it, reducing the person to an instrument of sexual pleasure. The one who pays sins gravely against himself: he violates the chastity to which his Baptism pledged him and defiles his body, the temple of the Holy Spirit. Prostitution is a social scourge. It usually involves women, but also men, children, and adolescents. (The latter two cases involve the added sin of scandal.) While it is always gravely sinful to engage in prostitution, the imputability of the offense can be attenuated by destitution, blackmail, or social pressure (n. 2355).

5. Regarding incest and the sexual abuse of children, the *CCC* says:

> *Incest* designates intimate relations between relatives or in-laws within a degree that prohibits marriage between them. St. Paul stigmatizes this especially grave offense: "It is actually reported that there is immorality among you ... for a man is living with his father's wife. . . . In the name of the Lord Jesus ... you are to deliver this man to Satan for the destruction of the flesh. . . ." Incest corrupts family relationships and marks a regression toward animality (n. 2388).
>
> Connected to incest is any sexual abuse perpetrated by adults on children or adolescents entrusted to their care. The offense is compounded by the scandalous harm done to the physical and moral integrity of the young, who will remain scarred by it all their lives; and the violation of responsibility for their upbringing. (n. 2389).

6. This rhythmic experience is called "undulation," from the Latin word *unda*, meaning wave.

7. "The forms taken by modesty vary from one culture to another. Everywhere, however, modesty exists as an intuition of the spiritual dignity proper to man. It is born with the awakening consciousness of being a subject. Teaching modesty to children and adolescents means awakening in them respect for the human person" (*CCC*, n. 2524).

CHAPTER 9

The Problem of Masturbation

Because pornography abounds in our society, certain forms of distorted sexual activity have been defended as justifiable or at least morally acceptable. One of these is masturbation. The *Catechism of the Catholic Church* defines masturbation as "the deliberate stimulation of the genital organs in order to derive sexual pleasure" (n. 2352).

This is a difficulty that many priests and spiritual directors unfortunately will not deal with today. Sometimes it is simply excused with the phrase "it's natural," the presumption being that most people at some time or another experience this behavior. To tell someone seeking counsel about masturbation or even mentioning it as a sin during confession, "Don't worry about it, it's no problem," is tantamount to a person with severe stomach pains being told by a doctor, "Don't worry about it, most people, at one time or another in their lives, get severe stomach pains."

Such answers are no help to those who suffer, whether from the stomach pains in the case of those who go to a doctor, or from the extreme guilt, confusion, fear and frustration of those who seek help from a spiritual director or confessor for the problem of masturbation.

The Church has consistently taught that there is a moral significance to masturbation, namely, that it is a grave moral disorder and must be corrected. This does not deny that there might be subjective factors present which may lessen personal. freedom and, therefore, responsibility and guilt on the part of certain individuals who fall into this behavior. Examples of some factors would be obsessive-compulsive behavior, deeply rooted habit, or a certain marked adolescent immaturity.[1]

A person struggling with the difficulty of masturbation has a right to be helped with his or her difficulties. To ignore the issue doesn't solve it; to expect it to go away on its own is like the idea of the ostrich burying its head in the sand in the face of danger. Such a person can and should be helped and guided by the solid principles of Church teaching.[2]

What follows is a clear summary of the Church's teaching in regard to masturbation:

> The traditional Catholic doctrine that masturbation constitutes a grave moral disorder is often called into doubt or expressly denied today. It is said that psychology and sociology show that it is a normal phenomenon of sexual development, especially among the young. It is stated that there is real and serious fault only in the measure the subject deliberately indulges in solitary pleasure closed in on self, because in this case, the act would be radically opposed to the loving communion of persons of different sex which some hold is what is principally sought in the use of the sexual faculty.
>
> This opinion is contradictory to the teaching and pastoral practice of the Catholic Church. Whatever the force of certain arguments of a biological and philosophical nature, which have sometimes been used by theologians, in fact, both the magisterium of the Church—in the course of a constant tradition—and the moral sense of the faithful have declared that masturbation is an intrinsically and seriously disordered act.
>
> The main reason is that, whatever the motive for

acting in this way, the deliberate use of the sexual faculty outside normal conjugal [i.e., marital] relations essentially contradicts the finality [i.e., purpose] of the faculty. For it lacks the sexual relationship called for by the moral order, namely, the relationship which realizes "the full sense of mutual self giving and human procreation in the context of true [married] love."

All deliberate exercise of sexuality must be reserved to this regular [marital] relationship. Even if it cannot be proved that Scripture condemns this sin [i.e., masturbation] by name, the tradition of the Church has rightly understood it to be condemned in the New Testament when the latter speaks of "impurity," "unchasteness," and other vices contrary to chastity and continence (*Persona Humana: Declaration on Certain Questions Concerning Sexual Ethics*, n. 9, Congregation for the Doctrine of the Faith, hereafter referred to as *Declaration*).

The erroneous teaching that masturbation can be justifiable or at least in itself not sinful has led many people to do nothing about overcoming the habit of masturbation. This has certainly done unfortunate harm to their spiritual lives. It is important for everyone, but especially for celibates, to deal with this difficulty. A person gains many spiritual benefits by resisting the temptation to masturbate, and even more so by overcoming the habit of it.

MASTURBATION IS "NAMELESS SEX"

Due to human weakness, masturbation has always been a concern. However, pornography has increased its frequency today among both men and women. Once pornography arouses sexual pleasure and desire, masturbation frequently occurs (among both married and celibate persons alike) as a means of achieving sexual gratification.

Like pornography, masturbation is "nameless sex."

Instead of the Christian marriage ideal of husband and wife expressing mutual love to one another, masturbation has no person to receive this expression. Masturbation negatively affects both married and celibate persons in their total psycho sexual make-up: physical, emotional, and spiritual.

Negative Effects on Married Persons

Physically, the act of masturbation is not directed toward anyone else. The sexual act is deprived of its natural capacity to express one's self-giving (self-donation) to another person. It closes the person in on himself or herself. It becomes merely a physical, self-centered act of self-gratification. Emotionally, masturbation lacks all loving, all caring for and sharing with another person. This negatively affects both spouses. On the part of the spouse who practices masturbation, he or she usually senses that it takes something away from their unique focus on their spouse, and it hinders the giving of the marital gift of self-donation. On the other hand, if the other spouse knows that his or her partner is doing this, they instinctively feel that that spouse is withholding something essential to the true marital covenant. Masturbation is often the beginning of alienation and loss of affection between spouses; it easily becomes a contributing factor to marital infidelity as well as to separation and divorce.

Spiritually, masturbation in a marriage violates the promises the spouses have made before God to share their mutual love in a manner faithful to God's commandments. It is also a disrespect and abuse of one's own body, which St. Paul called the "temple of the Holy Spirit:"

> Do you not know that your body is a temple of the Holy Spirit within you, which you have from God? You are not your own; you were bought with a price. So glorify God in your body. (1 Cor 6:19-20)

Negative Effects on Celibates

It is easy to see how masturbation negatively affects a celibate person in these same three ways. Physically, it fosters immature and immoral genital behavior, using sexual pleasure for mere physical gratification. If a habit of masturbation is formed, it can be very difficult to overcome later on.

Emotionally, the person becomes increasingly focused on his or her own needs and wants. Instead of becoming freer to love others, to care for them, or reach out to them, the celibate person becomes locked into a growing narcissism. As the practice of masturbation increases, love and concern for others proportionately decrease.

Spiritually, the celibate finds himself or herself in conflict with the commitment made to God. It brings a sense of guilt, a morbid preoccupation with sex, and often leaves the celibate somewhat depressed. The joy and peace of the Holy Spirit cannot exist in the human heart in such circumstances. It verifies the words of St. Paul that the flesh and the Spirit are directly opposed (cf. Gal 5:17).

TWO INSIGHTS INTO THE DIFFICULTY

Anyone wishing to live a chaste celibate life usually must struggle, to a greater or lesser degree, against tendencies and temptations toward masturbation. Two insights can give general help in the struggle.

Tensions Can Cause Difficulties

One very important point to keep in mind is that masturbation may be used as a means of dealing with tension and anxiety. Where some people might turn to alcohol or drugs to numb their inner pain, other people turn to masturbation. A big concern is that in neither case are the actual root-causes of the tensions or problems being dealt with. Consequently, the tensions and problems remain. Furthermore, those who practice masturbation usually experience guilt as a result of the behavior.

This situation is comparable to the story of a man who, under the weight of many personal problems, was down and out and feeling very sorry for himself. As he was walking by a bar, he saw a big sign in the window. It read: "Come on in! Cheer up! Things could be worse!" So he went in, he cheered up, and, sure enough, things got worse!

Masturbation is not only a moral disorder (sin), but is also an immature escape from dealing with problems and tensions, as is resorting to drinking or drugs. It is important for everyone to learn to deal with tensions in a healthy manner so as to alleviate the desire or compulsion to resort to masturbation. This is all part of the process of emotional and spiritual maturation. Both the ability to face reality (dealing with the problems causing the tensions) and to delay immediate gratification (the self-control needed to resist the temptation for immediate sexual pleasure) are signs of this maturation.

The Need to Move Out of Self-Centeredness

As human beings mature, we tend to move away from self-centeredness (which is characteristic of infants and young children) and move out toward others. Psychologists call this moving out toward others "altruism."[3] This means that as we mature, we develop not only an awareness of others, but also a respect for them and for their rights, as well as a concern for their needs. Therefore, true maturity always leads us out of narcissistic self-centeredness and directs us toward others. The Christian virtue of charity builds on altruism and enables us to love, give, forgive, share, sacrifice for others, and so on.

Masturbation, on the other hand, by keeping the person's focus on the self, stunts this process of altruism. Therefore, as already stated, masturbation can keep a person locked into the prison of self-centeredness and block growth toward truly caring (altruistic) love. It is interesting that many people, as they mature and develop a sense of reaching out to others in true love and concern, often find that previous difficulty with masturbation, even if it was habitual, will begin to diminish with time. Part of this is due to the fact that inner tensions lessen while authentic concern for others increases. It also may reflect the fact that in giving to others or doing good for them, a person experiences a certain satisfaction and even joy which helps to offset the morbid sadness and self-preoccupation that often accompany habitual masturbation.

CHOOSING CELIBACY, CONTROLLING MASTURBATION

If a person who is considering the choice of celibacy is struggling with habitual or compulsive masturbation, it is important that he or she find a good and caring confessor and spiritual director. Being open about this difficulty in confession can be a great help. Such persons should especially avoid the extremes of either simply excusing masturbation altogether as if it were of no account at all, or of making of it the most horrendous catastrophe. The *Declaration* provides a helpful, balanced approach here:

> Sociological surveys are able to show the frequency of this disorder (masturbation) according to the places, populations, or circumstances studied. In this way, facts are discovered, but facts do not constitute a criterion for judging the moral value of human acts. The frequency of the phenomenon in question is certainly to be linked with man's innate weakness following original sin; but it is also to be linked with a loss of a sense of God, with the corruption of morals engendered by the commercialization of vice, with the unrestrained licentiousness of so many public

entertainments and publications as well as with the neglect of modesty, which is the guardian of chastity.

On the subject of masturbation, modern psychology provides much valid and useful information for formulating a more equitable judgment on moral responsibility and for orienting pastoral action. Psychology helps one to see how the immaturity of adolescence (which can sometimes persist after that age), psychological imbalance, or habit can influence behavior, diminishing the deliberate character of the act and bringing about a situation whereby, subjectively, there may not always be serious fault. But, in general, the absence of serious responsibility must not be presumed; this would be to misunderstand peoples' moral capacity (n. 9).

Masturbation is a problem that can and should be dealt with. As will be developed further on, it requires fidelity to prayer (especially a deep Eucharistic devotion) and daily seeking of the intercession and protection of our Blessed Lady.

Struggling with temptations and problems such as masturbation can help develop within the celibate person a great confidence in God and in His mercy. The individual must learn to be patient, for progress can and will come if one is determined. Patience, in turn, helps to build humility which is the necessary foundation for all virtues. When we recognize our weakness, we can turn to God and ask His strength, for He is drawn to the humble, whereas He resists the proud. Persevering at one's efforts and not giving in to discouragement, in spite of occasional lapses, is very important. If a person should fall into the difficulty, he or she should begin again to make the effort necessary to practice chastity. Regular and even frequent reception of the Sacrament of Reconciliation is a very important factor here. Success in the practice of chaste celibacy will come in due time with the help of God's grace.

Notes

1. The *CCC* addresses this point:

To form an equitable judgment about the subjects' moral responsibility and to guide pastoral action, one must take into account the affective immaturity, force of acquired habit, conditions of anxiety, or other psychological or social factors that lessen or even extenuate moral culpability (n. 2352).

2. The Catholic Church's teaching about the moral character of masturbation is presented in the ecclesial document *Persona Humana: Declaration on Certain Questions Concerning Sexual Ethics.* Issued on December 29, 1975, by the Sacred Congregation for the Doctrine of the Faith, it was approved by the Servant of God Pope Paul VI.

3. "Altruism" is from the Latin word *alter*, meaning the other or another (person). "Altruism" is the movement away from a self-centered or narcissistic focus on self to a focus on and concern for others.

CHAPTER 10

The Question of Homosexuality

Homosexual tendencies present certain questions and difficulties in regard to a vowed celibate commitment. Some solid Catholic books have been written on the general subject of homosexuality in recent years[1] and there is no intention to offer here a fully detailed presentation on the topic. Rather, the focus of this book will be limited to one important question: "Should a person with a homosexual orientation make a public vow of consecrated celibacy?"

RELEVANT PRINCIPLES OF CATHOLIC TEACHING

In order to answer this question properly, certain aspects of homosexuality must first be considered. It is important to look at some of the observations about homosexuality presented in three recent documents of the Vatican's Congregation for the Doctrine of the Faith and examine certain principles of Catholic moral teaching that are pertinent to the question presented.[2]

The first concern of the documents is to identify a contemporary liberal tendency to condone homosexual actions as morally permissible and justifiable, or even as morally good.

> At the present time, there are those who, basing themselves on observations in the psychological order, have begun to judge indulgently, and even to excuse completely, homosexual relations between certain people. This they do in opposition to the constant teaching of the Magisterium and to the moral sense of the Christian people (*Declaration*, n. 8).

The documents also clearly teach that homosexual acts are "intrinsically disordered." This means that such acts are in obvious conflict with the purposes for which God intended human sexual activity: Namely, genital sexual activity must only be expressed in a monogamous, heterosexual marriage and must always be an expression of mutual, self-giving love and open to new life. Therefore, while recognizing that persons who have a homosexual orientation, like all human persons, must be treated with Christian respect, love, and concern, these documents assert the Church's constant teaching that homosexual actions, lacking this God-given purpose, can never be morally justified.

> In the pastoral field, these homosexuals must certainly be treated with understanding and sustained in the hope of overcoming their personal difficulties and their inability to fit into society. Their culpability will be judged with prudence. But no pastoral method can be employed which would give moral justification to these acts on the grounds that they would be consonant with the condition of such people. For according to the objective moral order, homosexual relations are acts which lack an essential and indispensable finality. In Sacred Scripture, they are condemned as a serious depravity and even presented as the sad consequence of rejecting God (cf. Rom 1:24-27). This judgment of Scripture does not of course permit us to conclude that all those who suffer from this anomaly are personally responsible for it, but it does attest to the fact that homosexual acts are intrinsically disordered

and can in no case be approved of (*Declaration*, n. 8).

Homosexual orientation vs. Homosexual Lifestyle

Another important point the documents make is the distinction between a homosexual orientation (tendency) and homosexual acts (lifestyle). The Church clearly recognizes that a homosexual orientation is not of itself sinful. Many factors beyond the individual's control can produce this condition. However, the Church sees that such an orientation is a "disorder" since it is not consistent with the normal psycho-sexual development the Creator intended.

> An overly benign interpretation was given to the homosexual condition itself, some going so far as to call it neutral or even good . . . Although the particular inclination of the homosexual person is not a sin, it is a more or less strong tendency ordered toward an intrinsic moral evil; and thus the inclination itself must be seen as an objective disorder. Therefore, special concern and pastoral attention should be directed toward those who have this condition, lest they be led to believe that the living out of this orientation in homosexual activity is a morally acceptable option. It is not (*Some Considerations Concerning the Response to Lesiglative Proposals on the Non-Discrimination of Homosexual Persons* [*Considerations*], Congregation for the Doctrine of the Faith, n. 2, July 22, 1992).

Causes of a Homosexual Orientation

A final important teaching in the Vatican documents deals with both the causes and curability of a homosexual orientation. In keeping with sound Christian principles, there is a distinction between what might be called a transitory and therefore curable homosexual orientation, and a definitive and non-curable orientation. This is an extremely important distinction in regard to the question of a vowed celibate commitment; it must be explored further.

A distinction is drawn, and it seems with some reason, between homosexuals whose tendency comes from a false education, from a lack of normal sexual development, from habit, from bad example, or from some other similar causes, and is transitory or at least not incurable; and homosexuals who are definitively such because of some kind of innate instinct or a pathological constitution judged to be incurable. (*Declaration*, n. 8)

In regard to this second category, some people conclude that their tendency is so natural that it justifies, in their case, homosexual relations within a sincere communion of life and love analogous to marriage, insofar as such individuals feel incapable of enduring a solitary life. It should be pointed out that although we recognize the struggle and sacrifice such an individual may personally have to deal with, such a position is contrary to Catholic Church teaching and is morally unacceptable.

UNDERSTANDING HUMAN SEXUALITY

In the past it was common to define sexuality simply as "sex behavior." Actually, human sexuality takes in all aspects of a person, all that is included when one speaks of "masculinity" and "femininity." To answer the question of what is homosexuality, it is important to recognize some distinctions when speaking of human sexuality in general. There is a need to distinguish: (1) sexual identity, (2) gender identity, and (3) sexual role behavior.

"Sexual identity" is fundamentally a person's biological makeup, possessing either male or female genital organs. This is determined by the genes received at conception. Today, by prenatal testing, doctors can determine whether the child in the womb is a boy or a girl.

"Gender identity" is how a person thinks of himself or herself. Who am I? How do I think? Act? Behave? It is expressed by young children, for example, in emphatic statements such as: "Little boys don't do that!" or "Little girls dress like this!" Gender identity is usually set in children by age five. Many psychologists who work with people struggling with their gender identity theorize that disruption in the normal process of psycho-sexual development in young children can result in confusion about one's gender identity.[3]

"Sexual role behavior" refers to how people perceive that they should act in society. This is subdivided into two aspects. The first is "gender behavior." How am I, as a boy or as a girl, expected to act in society? For example, the male may feel expected to be tough, even "macho." The female may sense a need to be passive and to look like a fashion model. It is in this area that the current "gender revolution" has caused considerable confusion and conflict with certain accepted Christian norms and principles.[4]

It has been fashionable, under the guise of "sexual liberation," to speak of freeing women from the seemingly burdensome role of motherhood, with all its apparent lackluster boredom and drudgery, thus "liberating" them to compete for positions of power and prestige in the work world in traditionally male roles. But this has proven to be no guarantee of happiness and satisfaction as many "liberated women" have found out. People can change gender roles, but changing the roles does not change human nature.[5]

The second aspect of "sexual role behavior" refers to the desires and actions involved in. "genital sexual behavior." Because of the current confusion in "gender behavior," some men and women, especially among teens and young adults, have experienced confusion also in terms of their genital expression. This confusion has influenced the thinking which justifies homosexual genital behavior. It is argued that if gender behavior roles have so drastically changed, if it is now acceptable for men to perform roles that were once considered exclusively women's roles and for women to perform roles that were previously labeled as distinctively male roles, then genital, sexual roles have likewise changed. Some of those seeking to justify a homosexual lifestyle argue: If "gender behavior" can change, then "genital sexual behavior" can also change; if traditional social roles can differ, then traditional sexual partners can differ also. Needless to say, such a position is contrary to Catholic Church teaching and could never be morally justified.

Homosexuality and Society

Various factors have contributed to the blurring of the lines between masculinity and femininity. First, there is the general permissive atmosphere of today's society which accepts all sexual behavior without consideration of its moral quality. Add to this the widespread influence of pornography, a good deal of which caters to and advocates a homosexual lifestyle. There is also a deliberate effort to make homosexuality as acceptable in today's society as the sexual expression of conjugal love in marriage. Backed by a great deal of media support, active pro-gay and pro-lesbian groups have used political pressure to promote their lifestyle as legally and morally acceptable. At times, pressure has also been put on the Church to support changes which make homosexuality acceptable in society.

> There is an effort in some countries to manipulate the Church by gaining the often well-intentioned support of her pastors with a view to changing civil statutes and laws. This is done in order to conform to these pressure groups' concepts that homosexuality is at least a completely harmless, if not an entirely good, thing. Even when the practice of homosexuality may seriously threaten the lives and well-being of a large number of people, its advocates remain undeterred and refuse to consider the magnitude of the risks involved. . . (*Considerations*, n. 9)

JUDAEO-CHRISTIAN TEACHING

The widespread promotion of homosexuality today has made even more difficult the question of whether it hinders a call to committed celibacy.

There are some within the Church who see nothing morally wrong with homosexual behavior. Accordingly they do not see any difficulty with active homosexuals entering the priesthood or religious life, thereby taking the vow of celibacy. They argue that celibacy merely forbids heterosexual marriage.

But it has been clearly shown that Gospel celibacy not only involves the renunciation of marriage, it also obliges those who embrace it to observe the sixth and ninth commandments because of the virtue of religion. Homosexual acts in themselves are grave violations of that chastity proper to all Christians, and are sufficiently wrong to constitute matter for mortal sin. As already pointed out, this has been the constant and consistent teaching of Sacred Scripture and Catholic Tradition.

It seems evident that anyone who attempts to live as a sincere Catholic, yet finds himself or herself consistently participating in an active homosexual lifestyle because of weakness and perhaps long entrenched habit, should not yet attempt to make a vow of chaste celibacy. This would only add to their moral responsibility and probably aggravate a deep sense of guilt and shame. It would seem prudent and even necessary that, through such means as prayer, the Sacraments, and spiritual guidance, such a person first attain a measure of self-control over their genital behavior through self-discipline. Furthermore, this self-control should be tested over a period of several years. St. Paul gives us a powerful reminder of what it means to come to the Lord in our lives: "And those who belong to Christ Jesus have crucified the flesh with its passions and desires" (Gal 5:24).

UNDERSTANDING HOMOSEXUALITY

Homosexuality is more common among men than women, though lesbianism is increasing. Homosexuality is when a person's primary sexual desire is toward "bonding" (i.e., a strong emotional attraction to and/or physical union) with a person of one's own sex rather than the opposite sex (that is, heterosexuality).

A homosexual orientation can be caused by various factors. Many times, it is the result of the deprivation of same sex nurturing or same sex bonding in one's childhood. This often occurs in situations where the parent of the same sex is very weak or passive (so that no psychological bonding with the parent of one's own sex takes place; in other words, the boy cannot bond with his father). At the same time, if the parent of the opposite sex is overbearing or perhaps even consciously or unconsciously seductive, the child bonds with that parent.

Another factor is the experience of sexual abuse or molestation as a child, especially if it is of a homosexual nature. This is particularly hurtful before the age of puberty, and especially for boys, although girls who suffer childhood sexual abuse or even rape may consequently fear men and so turn to a person of their own sex for bonding.

Types of Homosexuality

Because there are different causes of homosexuality, different types can be distinguished. Here are four types.

(1) Situational Homosexuality

Situational homosexuality is when a person who normally prefers a partner of the opposite sex chooses to experience genital behavior with a person of the same sex because of their current situation (for example, being in prison and no one of the opposite sex is available).

(2) Incidental Homosexuality

Incidental homosexuality often occurs in adolescence and is usually due to curiosity (to see what such an experience is like) or is exploratory (a teenager or young adult who is uncertain of his or her own sexual identity performs a single or very limited number of homosexual actions to "test out" their orientation). Often, later on, there is a strong heterosexual development.

(3) Pseudo-Homosexuality

This occurs at a time, when the individual experiences a peak in his or her sexual desires and feelings. For a male, this usually happens in later adolescence (around 18-21 years of age). For a female, this usually occurs in her late 20s or early 30s. If the individual is restricted by their environment from the opposite sex at a time when these sexual desires and feelings are at their height, he or she may turn to a person of the same sex to engage in genital behavior. If the environment changes and there are persons of the opposite sex present, the person will probably experience a heterosexual attraction. However, it is not uncommon for such persons to be left with "scars" from the homosexual experience and question his or her true sexual identity: "Am I homosexual or not?" They may, later on, experience further attractions to persons of the same sex.

All three of these types of homosexuality are considered "curable," that is, the person's orientation can be readjusted to a heterosexual one. It should be noted that the first and second types of homosexuality mentioned here usually do not present a permanent difficulty to a lifelong celibate commitment, provided the person matures in their psycho-sexual development and grows in self-control by the virtue of chastity. The third type will perhaps require some counseling in addition to solid spiritual direction to work out residual problems of sexual identity confusion. This may take some time and a good deal of personal effort, making postponement of a public vow of celibacy advisable.

(4) Real Homosexuality

The fourth type is what could be referred to as "real" homosexuality. In this case, the individual realizes at a very young age, even around eight or nine years old, that he or she does not have the same interests and attractions as other boys or girls. The differences often become more noticeable as the person develops through adolescence and young adulthood. For example, a heterosexual male generally prefers the company of other men for association, but of a woman for genital activity. A gay male often prefers the company of women for association, but of another man for genital behavior. A similar difference can also be noted between heterosexual and lesbian females.

Real homosexuality is generally considered "not curable." Especially if a person has been active in the homosexual lifestyle for a long period of time, it can present serious difficulties to vowed celibacy. What has already been stated of "pseudo-homosexuality" and the advisability of delaying a public vow of celibate chastity applies even more so to those persons struggling with "real homosexuality." And, obviously, if the person is still "active," not only would it be most imprudent to obligate one's self to live chaste celibacy, but the vow would lack honesty and integrity as long as any unchaste relationship continued.

> An individual's sexual orientation is generally not known to others unless he publicly identifies himself as having this orientation or unless some overt behavior manifests it. As a rule, the majority of homosexually oriented persons who seek to lead chaste lives do not publicize their sexual orientation...
>
> Homosexual persons who assert their homosexuality tend to be precisely those who judge homosexual behavior or lifestyle to be "either completely harmless, if not an entirely good thing" and hence worthy of public approval

(*Considerations*, n. 14).

At this point, the focal question of this chapter should be addressed. "Should a person with a homosexual orientation make a vow of celibacy?" It seems prudent to say that if persons in the first three categories succeed in gaining self-control through the practice of the virtue of chastity, they could prudently make at least a private vow of celibacy if they felt attracted to it.[6] As seen already, such a vow can help a person be constant in the determination to practice celibate chastity.

However, when it comes to making a public vow by entering the priesthood or religious life, certain other considerations should first be made. This is because there will be many new responsibilities, in fact, a whole new lifestyle, connected with these vocations. One point that seems very important is that these persons should first test their ability, with God's grace, to live in chaste celibacy over a sufficiently long period of time.

The document from the Vatican's Congregation for Institutes of Consecrated Life and Societies of Apostolic Life, *Directives in Formation in Religious Institutes* (*Directives*), addresses this. Speaking of the need for future religious to appreciate the unique contributions and roles of male and female sexuality in the divine plan of creation and salvation, it states:

> In this context reasons must be given and understood to explain why those who do not seem to be able to overcome their homosexual tendencies or who maintain that it is possible to adapt a third way, "living in an ambiguous state between celibacy and marriage," . . . must be dismissed from the religious life. (n. 39)

Other considerations that must be made by those pursuing the priesthood and religious life include dealing realistically with the likelihood of (1) living in community with persons of the same sex (e.g., in a seminary, convent, rectory); (2) working with children and teenagers (who can be easy targets for sexual gratification in moments of weakness); and (3) the possibility of giving public scandal (since priests and religious are "public persons" in the Church community). The guidance of a good confessor and spiritual director is invaluable in this discernment process. These factors will be discussed in more detail later in this chapter.

WHAT IF THE ANSWER IS NO?

It may well happen that a person who has a real homosexual orientation and who is asking the question, "Should I make a public vow of celibacy as a religious or priest?" comes honestly to the answer, "no." If the individual realizes that either the probability of perseverance is not realistic, or the likelihood of sinful patterns of homosexual behavior emerging is great, or the risk of grave scandal is likely, they would have to conclude that they are not being called to a public vocation and a public vow in the Church. We would have to admire the honesty and courage of such a conclusion, while recognizing the extreme pain it is likely to produce.

Some people are able to see more easily the hand of God in such circumstances, and can live with the conclusion without a great deal of turmoil. For many others, this may not be the case. For quite a number of years, I have been involved in both vocation and formation work as a religious. I have dealt with young people who were applying to enter religious life and were discerning the signs of God's call, as well as others who were already in the early years of their formative process, testing the authenticity of their call. I have known cases where candidates may have been denied entrance or young religious have been asked to leave because of difficulties experienced in the area of homosexuality.

It certainly can be a great disappointment, especially when the person's heart was set on a vocation to the priesthood or religious life. Most come to accept the disappointment to some degree, but a few experience deep hurt and anger. To deal realistically with an honest answer of "no," two factors should be kept in mind. First, if God is genuinely calling an individual to a public celibate commitment, He must give all the graces necessary to fulfill it properly, with some measure of joy and peace. This is why it has been the Church's constant practice to look for the "signs of a vocation" or call from God. If something essential is lacking or obviously questionable, we have to conclude that God is not actually calling this individual, at least not at this particular time. If the individual is seeking sincerely to do God's will and not his or her own (for example, to enter for self-centered reasons, such as prestige, security, acceptance, and the like), then he or she would be disposed, to some degree at least, to accept God's will as manifest in these circumstances.

Secondly, a person who loves the Church—and the good of others—would be strongly motivated to avoid whatever could be a cause of infidelity to assumed responsibilities (where others would be hurt by neglect) or scandal (where bad example could lead others into sin, or at least cause the esteem of the Church and her God-given mission to be unjustly diminished). The Church, based on the experience of her long history, has always followed the principle: If it is a matter of the general good of the Church or the personal good of a private individual, the good of the Church must take precedence.

ORIENTATION VS. ACTIVITY

Some persons may have a real homosexual orientation but never "act it out" or even acknowledge the orientation. Sometimes, this is due to the fear of being known as a homosexual. This is not a good or sufficient safeguard against later homosexual activity, since the fear may give way under the power of attraction or curiosity. However, if a person acknowledges that this is their orientation but has consistently chosen to practice chastity for love of God and respect for the demands of chastity, such a person may have sufficient self-control for a private vow of celibacy.

As for entrance into the priesthood or religious life, the resolve to live celibacy faithfully must be proven. This is best seen a little later in life, perhaps in one's thirties. The reason is that living in a religious community (or seminary or rectory) means living constantly with persons toward whom one may come to feel strong sexual attractions; the constant battle to keep these powerful attractions under control will consume most of the person's energy. It could prove to be a continuous act of heroism and a veritable martyrdom. As a result, there might be little or no energy or enthusiasm left to live the other demands of consecrated life with a positive attitude and a joyous heart.

THE QUESTION OF ANGER

Many homosexual persons must also deal with a fair amount of anger in their lives. This anger often stems from a lack of bonding in earlier life and may be directed toward one or both parents or toward one's siblings. In fact, most uncontrolled or compulsive genital activity is a sign of a lack of certain affective needs having been met. This includes the need for acceptance, love, belonging, protection from harm or from feelings of insecurity, and the need to learn appropriate ways to relate to others on a social and emotional level. This anger must be dealt with and ways to fulfill these needs in a healthy, Christian manner must be learned. Inner healing, forgiveness and gentleness are usually needed to deal with hurts, deprivation, and resentments from the past.

Anger at God

There may also be anger at God and the Church. People

feel angry at God when He doesn't meet their expectations, or when He allows them to experience disagreeable or painful things, even if they themselves brought about the circumstances that caused these difficulties.[7] Anger at God is probably more common than most religious people suspect.

People with a homosexual orientation may feel angry at God for allowing their homosexual condition (whatever the causes of that condition might be). This anger must be countered by patient acceptance of what God has permitted, and not caused, trusting that He will somehow, in some way, be able to bring us to happiness in spite of it all. St. Paul assures us (cf. Rom 8:28) that God can work all things toward some good as long as we earnestly love Him and trust the often mysterious workings of His Divine Providence.

As Cardinal Newman once wrote: "God does nothing in vain . . . He knows what He is about!"

Anger at the Church

More significant may be anger at the Church. This anger is quite evident today in secular society, which tends to make the Church the source and the scapegoat for all problems. The secular press has made it a point to publicize Catholic clergy and religious who fail in the area of sexual behavior. As harmful and tragic as these failings are, especially pedophilia,[8] perhaps the failings are given disproportionate attention because the Church is one of the few voices in today's permissive society that still speaks out against injustice and immorality; in this case, the Church speaks out against homosexuality and rejects it as morally unacceptable.

When people living in a homosexual lifestyle vent anger at the Church, they may be projecting feelings of anger actually erected toward themselves. Many active gays and lesbians are earnestly struggling against the very sexual behavior which the Church condemns in such strong language; yet, in spite of their best efforts they keep falling into it. This in itself may cause them to feel rejected by the Church they love deeply.

This anger can only be healed by the recognition of God's mercy. As the anger is healed, the individual becomes freer to accept God's mercy (thereby helping to remove or at least reduce feelings of shame) and to recognize that the Church does accept them as persons with the sacredness common to all God's people.

HOMOSEXUALITY AND
THOSE ALREADY COMMITTED

A final area of concern is for those who are already committed to a publicly vowed life of celibacy as a priest or a religious but who have come to realize that they have a real homosexual orientation. A few considerations may be helpful. A primary consideration is the individual's initial motivation for choosing celibacy. Proper motivation, as we have already seen, requires a choice made in freedom and out of love and based on true supernatural reasons. Wrong or inadequate motivation would distort the purpose for choosing celibacy. For a young person with a homosexual orientation, there is potentially present the inadequate motive to enter the priesthood or the religious life in order to conceal their orientation. Since they would be expected to live celibately, there would be no questions asked as to why they never married, or even dated. If a priest or religious suspects that such was their initial motivation, it is absolutely essential to substitute a motive of supernatural faith, such as love for Christ and for the least of His brothers and sisters. A compassionate and qualified spiritual director is helpful for this process. This is to set one's life of celibacy on a solid foundation. One thing is the motivation with which a person begins; quite another thing is the motivation with which one continues and perseveres to the end by God's grace.

Another important point is whether the priest or religious

is currently involved in homosexual activity. If so, this must end if the person is to experience spiritual growth and the healing grace of the Holy Spirit. Giving up all genital sexual activity and striving to attain purity of mind and body is essential to celibate living in and for Christ. The sincere effort to live a chaste, spiritual life can produce marvelous effects, especially the growth of inner freedom and joy.

A third consideration is whether there is a danger of scandal. If so, the individual may need to seek immediate counseling. A "time off" period to receive in-depth therapy to help heal ongoing internal conflicts may also be necessary.

Many individuals with a homosexual orientation have gained the self-discipline needed to live good and holy lives in the service of the Lord and His people. Sometimes, two persons of homosexual orientation, even if one or both were formerly active in the lifestyle, after a conversion experience, can actually help one another to live chaste lives. This is especially the case where these two individuals have clear moral goals and strong spiritual motivation. Trusting in God's grace, these individuals have come to realize that the Lord who began good things in them will bring them to completion (cf. Phil 1:6) with their generous and faithful. and, many times, heroic cooperation.

Notes

1. Two helpful books on the subject of homosexuality, which contain further useful bibliographies, are *The Courage to be Chaste* by Fr. Benedict Groeschel, CFR (Paulist Press: New York/Mahwah, 1985) and *The Homosexual Person* by Fr. John Harvey, OSFS (Ignatius Press: San Francisco, 1987).

2. These Vatican documents are (in chronological order): (1) *Declaration on Certain Questions Concerning Sexual Ethics* (1975); (2) *Letter to Bishops of the Catholic Church on the Pastoral Care of Homosexual Persons* (*Letter*) (1986); (3)

Some Considerations Concerning the Response to Legislative Proposals on the Non-Discrimination of Homosexual Persons (1992).

3. Two authors presenting research and theories on this topic are Elizabeth Moberly (*Homosexuality: A New Christian Ethic*, Greenwood, SC: Attic Press, 1983) and Joseph Nicolosi (*Reparative Therapy of Male Homosexuality: A New Clinical Approach*, Northvale, NJ: Aronson Books 1991).

4. This is reflected in the Vatican document *Directives on Formation in Religious Institutes*. In the section "Sexuality and Formation," it speaks of the necessity for anyone entering religious life today to respect male and female differences.

> Young people today have often grown up in such integrated situations that boys and girls are not helped to know and appreciate the wealth and limitations of their respective gender. Formation in this area is particularly important due to apostolic contacts of all kinds and the greater collaboration which has begun between religious men and women as well as present cultural currents. Early desegregation and close and frequent cooperation do not necessarily guarantee maturity in the relationships between the two sexes. It is necessary to actively promote this maturity and to strengthen it with a view toward formation for the observance of chastity.
>
> Moreover men and women must become aware of their specific place in the plan of God, of the unique contribution which respectively they should make to the work of salvation. Future religious should thus be offered the possibility of reflecting on the role of sexuality in the divine plan of creation and salvation. . . (n. 39)

5. *Directives* states this point in clear and positive terms. Speaking of the formation of women for religious life, the document reads:

> A "penetrating and accurate consideration of

the anthropological foundation for masculinity and femininity will aim at clarifying woman's personal identity in relation to man, that is, a diversity yet mutual complementarity, not only as it concerns roles to be held and functions to be performed, but also, and more deeply, as it concerns her nature and meaning as a person" (*Christifideles Laici*, n. 50, apostolic exhortation, Pope John Paul II, December 30, 1988). This history of religious life bears witness to the fact that many women, within the cloister or in the world, have found there an ideal place for the service of God and others, conditions favorable to the expansion of their own femininity and, as a consequence, to a fuller understanding of their own identity. This growth in depth is to be pursued with the help of theological reflection and "the help that can come from different human sciences and cultures" (n. 41).

6. There must also be demonstrated a freedom from "dependent" relationships with others, especially of homosexual orientation, on whom one might tend to lean as emotional crutches. This will be further developed in the following chapter on friendship.

7. I remember reading about a young lady who became angry with God for allowing her to become pregnant when she had sexual relations with her boyfriend before marriage!

8. A pedophile is a person who is attracted to children as the object of his or her sexual desires, fantasies, and actions.

Chapter 11

Friendship:
A Gift Supporting Celibacy

The importance of friendships in every human life is reflected in an old saying: "Show me your friends, and I will tell you what you are!" We generally attract friends with whom we share certain values and beliefs; in turn, others attract us as friends by who they are. This mutual influence ranks, after that of our parents, as one of the most significant we will ever experience. It can affect us for better or for worse for the remainder of our lives.

THE PRICELESS VALUE OF TRUE FRIENDS

The gift of friendship is one of God's greatest gifts to us. In Sacred Scripture, the Old Testament writer Sirach describes friendship as a priceless "treasure" and points out the many great blessings that flow from it:

> A faithful friend is a sturdy shelter:
> he that has found one has found a treasure.

> There is nothing so precious as a faithful friend,
>   and no scales can measure his excellence.
> A faithful friend is an elixir of life;
>   and those who fear the Lord will find him.
> Whoever fears the Lord directs his friendship aright,
>   for as he is, so is his neighbor also (Sir 6:14-17).

Like a "sturdy shelter," a friend is always there for us, in good times and in bad. A friend shares in a special way in our lives. Our friends become part of us, almost another self, an "alter ego." With friends, we experience a give and take that mutually enriches our lives; what we receive from them enhances our lives, and they in turn receive from us.

This is why there is a good deal of truth in the popular saying: "Friends double our joys and divide our sorrows!" The joys of our lives seem to multiply when we share them with those who care about us and who are ready to rejoice with us in our blessings, accomplishments, and significant celebrations. Just to share these joys with friends increases their meaning to us.

On the other hand, when times are difficult, true friends show themselves to be like a "sturdy shelter," able to hold up and give us some protection from the storms and trials of life that threaten us. When we unburden our struggles, fears, and sorrows with friends, their loving concern makes them feel lighter. Realizing that someone else cares about how we are doing or how things are turning out gives us renewed courage to bear difficulties with patience and not give up. Remembering that our friends in Christ are keeping us in prayer in difficult times is also a real. source of consolation. Friends truly divide our sorrows because they carry our burdens with us.

A CAUTION AGAINST FALSE FRIENDS

Just as everything that glitters is not gold, so every

friendship is not necessarily a true or healthy one. In the same section where Sirach spoke of true friends, he adds a warning against false friends:

> For there is a friend who is such
>   at his own convenience,
> but will not stand by you
>   in your day of trouble.
> And there is a friend who changes into an enemy,
>   and will disclose a quarrel to your disgrace.
> And there is a friend who is a table companion,
>   but will not stand by you in your day of trouble.
> In prosperity he will make himself your equal,
>   and be bold with your servants;
> but if you are brought low
>   he will turn against you,
> and will hide himself from your presence. (Sir 6:8-12)

The first kind of false friend is one who is a friend "when it suits him." This is a person who is a friend for the sake of convenience. Such a person approaches friendship, albeit unconsciously, with attitudes like: "What can I gain from this friendship? How can this person be useful to me?" These people are friends according to their moods: if and when they feel like it! False friends also include "fair weather friends," or, as Sirach writes, friends who "will not stand by you in your day of trouble." These persons stay near as long as no demand or inconvenience is put upon them; however, when difficulties arise, they suddenly "disappear."

True friendship is constant. It rises above the ups and downs of mood swings that characterize immature friendshiPs False friendship is given conditionally: "As long as no demands are made on me, I'll be your friend." True friendships, instead, are not selfishly conditional.

Another kind of false friend is described as one "who

changes into an enemy." This is a disloyal friend who ends up betraying the other's confidence. This betrayal can hurt deeply, because the most personal information, shared with them in utter confidence, is told openly to others. This includes especially any difficulties that caused the two friends to part: Sirach describes the false friend as he or she who "discloses a quarrel to your disgrace." A bond of trust forms between true friends. To offend that trust is to destroy something sacred. It amounts to the highest form of betrayal. The pain of this betrayal is echoed in the Psalms:

> It is not an enemy who taunts me—
>   then I could bear it;
> it is not an adversary who deals
>   insolently with me—
> then I could hide form him.
>   But it is you, my equal,
> my companion, my familiar friend.
>   We used to hold sweet converse together;
> within God's house we walked in fellowship.
> (Ps 55:12-14)

Jesus suffered this disloyalty and betrayal at the hands of one of His own apostles, Judas Iscariot. In fact, when Judas was about to give the signal of betrayal to the Jewish authorities and Temple police in the Garden of Gethsemane, Our Lord made a last attempt to reach out to him, calling him "friend" (Matt 26:50). He also tried to show Judas his treason in using a kiss, a sign of friendship, for betrayal: "Judas, would you betray the Son of Man with a kiss" (Luke 22:48)? This suffering from a disloyal friend must have added much anguish to the sufferings of the Lord's passion.

FRIENDSHIP IS A FORM OF LOVE

Friendship is one of the chief forms of love. Unfortunately, in English we have only the one word to express many different aspects and forms of love. The Greek language was much more precise. They had four different words for love because they were able to distinguish between four different aspects or kinds of love.

One Greek word for love was *storge*. This meant affectionate love, especially familial affection. It was the affection of parents for their children and of children for their parents. It was an affection rooted in the bonds of birth and blood.

Eros was another word for love in Greek. It was used mainly to speak of sexual love. It included not only the physical expression of love, but also the sense of "being in love" with one's spouse. *Eros*-love is viewed basically as a love of utility or usefulness: A person or thing is loved if they satisfy or benefit me. From *eros* comes the English word "erotic" which has the rather negative connotation of selfishly arousing passionate or lustful drives and desires.

Another word for love in Greek is *agape*. This word was rarely used in classical Greek. However, the early Church adapted it to express the distinctively Christian form of love, a charity open to all people. It is a totally giving, all-embracing, and self-sacrificing love. It is not limited to family or friends, but includes the charity that loves strangers and even enemies for the love of God. It is the main word for love in the New Testament. It is the love Christ taught us to have for one another as He had for us.

The final Greek word for love, the one that we will focus on, is *philia*. It means a close, warm, loving affection. It refers to the kind of love found in a stable and ongoing relationship with someone who is near and dear. It was sometimes used to speak of the love of husband and wife, but it was especially applied to the love of friendship. It was a love involving a mutual giving and receiving for the sake of the person loved.

WHAT IS FRIENDSHIP?

Psychologists point out that there is an element of mystery in the attraction of friends. Why is it, for example, that out of ten people I know well at school, at work, or in the neighborhood, I may feel attracted in friendship toward only two or three of them? Furthermore, what attracts people to one another in friendship is not known for sure: Some say, "opposites attract," while others hold that, "like attracts like."

One thing for certain about true friendships is that they must be entered into freely; friendship can never be forced on anyone. Teenagers often become upset and may even anguish over the fact that they want a special person to be their friend, but that other person does not want to respond as a friend. The love of friendship can only be freely given and freely received.

There is a story connected with a famous painting by Holman Hunt that illustrates this point. The painting portrays Jesus knocking at a door. When the artist finished his masterpiece, he invited friends in to view the painting and offer any comments. Everyone greatly admired it, but one person finally mentioned that there was a slight error in the painting. He observed that the door Jesus was knocking on did not have a door knob. How was Jesus to open the door when the person inside responded, "Come in?" The artist said that he deliberately painted the door without a door knob. His explanation was that this represented the door to the human heart. The only way it could be opened was by the person freely opening it from the inside. Even Jesus could not force His way into the heart and friendship of others; we must freely accept Him as our friend. It is the same for every other true friendship.

THE CHARACTERISTICS OF TRUE FRIENDSHIP

St. Thomas Aquinas teaches that true friendships require five elements.

First, the love in friendship is a love of benevolence, not of utility. It was already pointed out that *eros*-love is a love of utility because it uses people and things for its own satisfaction or benefit. It is a self-centered love. *Eros*-love is not *philia*-love.

Benevolence, on the other hand, is from the Latin words *bene* (well) and *volens* (wishing), which mean "wishing someone well." Benevolence is a ready disposition to assist or benefit others, not simply oneself.

The second quality of love in friendship is that it is mutual. This means that there is a reciprocal giving and receiving between the friends. When one or both friends permanently cease giving or receiving, the friendship is over. This quality of mutual love also implies that the love forms a stable relationship. This distinguishes friends from mere acquaintances, whom we get to know or interact with only in passing.

Third, the love of friendship tends to manifest itself in actions and not just in words. This could take the form of gestures of kindness, remembrances (for example, birthday greetings and anniversaries), help, or even the supreme sacrifice of one's life given for one's friends. Our Lord said that there can be no greater love than to give one's own life for a friend (cf. John 15:13).

A fourth characteristic of the love of friendship is that it tends to unite the two friends into one being. An example of this quality is expressed in a sermon by St. Gregory of Nazianzen in which he speaks about his friendship with St. Basil the Great:

> When we acknowledged our friendship and recognized that our ambition was a life of true wisdom, we became everything to each other: we shared the same lodging, the same table, the same desires, the same goal. Our love for each other grew daily warmer and deeper. The same hope inspired

us: the pursuit of learning... We each looked on the other's success as his own... We seemed to be two bodies with a single spirit... In our case, each of us was in the other and with the other... (from a sermon by St. Gregory Nazianzen, bishop)

The fifth and final characteristic is likeness or similarity. The love of friendship tends to make friends become more like one another. For those whose friendships are rooted in Christ, as each grows in likeness to Christ, they also grow in likeness to each other. Again, the sermon of St. Gregory Nazianzen on his friendship with St. Basil gives us a clear example of this:

Our single object and ambition was virtue, and a life of hope in the blessings that are to come; we wanted to withdraw from this world before we departed from it. With this end in view we ordered our lives and all our actions. We followed the guidance of God's law and spurred each other on to virtue. If it is not too boastful to say, we found in each other a standard and rule for discerning right from wrong.

Different men have different names, which they owe to their parents or to themselves, that is, to their own pursuits and achievements. But our great pursuit, the great name we wanted, was to be Christians, to be called Christians. (*ibid.*)

JESUS AND FRIENDSHIP

Our Lord had friends, those close to Him whom He loved with a special affection. Some of His friends were Lazarus and his sisters, Martha and Mary (cf. John 11:3). Jesus would often go to their home enjoying a meal with them and sharing their friendship. Above all, our Lord expressed friendship for His twelve apostles. At the Last Supper, He explicitly called them "friends":

You are My friends if you do what I command you. No longer do I call you servants, for the servant does not know

what his master is doing; but I have called you friends, for all
that I have heard from My Father I have made known to you.
(John 15:14-15)

Up to this point in their following of Jesus, the apostles
had been as slaves (i.e., servants) and disciples (i.e., pupils).
Now, they were to enter into a new relationship with Him: They
were now His friends. This is, no doubt, a recognition of how
much they had grown in their knowledge, love and service of
the Lord.

We see this in the apostles' careful observance of the
teachings Jesus had commanded them to carry out. In turn,
our Lord shared with them on a new level: He made known
to them, as one friend to another, His personal knowledge of
the Father and the hidden mysteries the Father had revealed to
Him. As in all friendships, Jesus revealed His most personal and
cherished secrets to His friends.

Friendship with Jesus

Friendship with Jesus is the first and most essential
friendship for those who are celibate for the sake of the kingdom
of heaven. He shares with them the same friendship He shared
with the apostles. To secure this friendship, as did the apostles,
celibate Christians must be ready to do whatever He commands.
It must be a friendship expressed not primarily in words but in
deeds. In turn, Jesus will reveal the Father more deeply and
personally, along with a greater understanding of the mysteries
of the kingdom. He will do this by pouring forth the Holy Spirit
upon those committed to Him, for the Holy Spirit is His first
Gift to us (cf. Acts 2:38), the first fruits of the redemption (cf.
Rom 8:23).

Friendship with Others

If we could see Jesus, hear Him, touch Him, in a word,

experience His immediate presence, His friendship would be all-sufficient for us. It would fulfill our every affective need for love and acceptance. But, this friendship with Jesus is now lived only in faith. He is not seen; He has gone to prepare a place in His kingdom for all those who love and serve Him faithfully. But celibates, like all of Jesus' friends, need the affective support of human friendships as well. These are crucial to their total human and Christian growth and well-being.

Friendships help us grow by drawing us out of ourselves and toward others. By our awareness of others and reaching out to them, we break out of the prison of self-centeredness. This happens through *agape*-love, that Christian love Jesus taught us to share with all people, even the least of His brothers and sisters. *Agape*-love is a powerful expression of charity, a totally giving, self-sacrificing love. However, it is often shown primarily to strangers, like the hungry or homeless, or in isolated instances, as in an emergency. Oftentimes, it is a love taken for granted, or not reciprocated, as in the love of our enemies or the forgiveness of those who have wronged us. It is a giving of our human, yet God-inspired love. However, in many instances, there is no human response to *agape*-love.

The *philia*-love of friendship, instead, is a reciprocal love, with mutual giving and receiving. In friendship, we experience a return of love and acceptance which fulfills our affective needs. Furthermore, this type of friendship is a stable relationship. *Philia*-love can deepen over time, maturing in its level of giving, receiving, caring, and sharing. The love of a friend can challenge the other to grow, thus deepening selfawareness (i.e., I see my worth as a person from the love and acceptance my friend gives me) and awareness of others (i.e., I deepen my perception and awareness of the worth of my friend as my relationship grows with him or her).

COMPARISON WITH MARITAL FRIENDSHIP

Marital Friendship

Ideally, the love of friendship should naturally occur in marriage, especially in the Christian Sacrament of Matrimony. However, friendship in marriage cannot be assumed or taken for granted. Sometimes it is not *philia*-love that binds a couple together, but *eros*-love (i.e., sexual satisfaction or material benefit) or *storge*-love (i.e., love for the children) or, often in heroic situations, *agape*-love (i.e., a love "for better or for worse"). But where *philia*-love or friendship exists between spouses, it draws each partner out of himself or herself more fully. Each shares with the other their characteristic qualities of body and soul, mind and heart. For example, the husband may share his strength while the wife shares her tenderness; the wife may enrich the marriage with her gift of intuition, as the husband brings to it his logical reasoning.

Each partner fulfills and enriches the other. Their affective needs to give and receive, to love and to be loved, to accept and to be accepted, to possess and to be possessed, are mutually satisfied. Furthermore, this *philia*-love will be expressed in a holistic relationship, involving their physical, emotional, and spiritual make-up. This is the gift of marital intimacy. It is exclusive between the two of them, no one else having a right to what they have pledged to each other by their marriage vows. This is a gift and a pledge that sincere married couples guard most jealously.

Celibate Friendship

Celibates, on the other hand, have renounced this marital intimacy. They do not have a spouse with whom they share in a holistic way (i.e., physically, emotionally and spiritually) their mutual love and acceptance. Yet, they still retain their human need for affection, which means their need for a warm, human love, acceptance, and concern from others. This is at the heart of the celibate's need for true friendship.

A clear example of this need is found in the apostolic exhortation of Pope John Paul II, *I Will Give You Shepherds*. It deals with the vital need for the proper formation of priests in the difficult circumstances of today's society. In the section titled "Human Formation, the Basis of All Priestly Formation," the Holy Father stressed the need for future priests to develop their human qualities. This is necessary in order to achieve proper maturity and self-realization, but also to prepare the seminarian to carry out his future priestly ministry. To attain this goal, Pope John Paul II stresses the need to develop the personal capacity to relate to other people. He singles out "affective maturity"[1] as the most significant and decisive factor in priestly formation:

> "Affective maturity" presupposes an awareness that love has a sensual role in human life. In fact, as I have written in the encyclical *Redemptor Hominis*, "Man cannot live without love. He remains a being that is incomprehensible for himself, his life is meaningless, if love is not revealed to him, if he does not encounter love, if he does not experience it and make it his own, if he does not participate intimately in it" (n. 44).

The Holy Father then explains that this need for affective maturity can be met by a proper education in human sexuality, which includes and highlights true "friendship":

> Education for responsible love and the affective maturity of the person are totally necessary for those who, like the priests, are called to celibacy, that is, to offer with the grace of the Spirit and the free response of one's own will, the whole of one's love and care to Jesus Christ and to His Church. In view of the commitment to celibacy, affective maturity should bring to human relationships of serene friendship and deep brotherliness, a strong, lively, and personal love for Jesus Christ. As the Synod Fathers have written: "A love for Christ, which overflows into a dedication to everyone, is of the

greatest importance in developing affective maturity. Thus, the candidate, who is called to celibacy, will find in affective maturity a firm support to live chastity in faithfulness and joy.

Since the charism of celibacy, even when it is genuine and has proved itself, leaves man's affections and his instinctive impulses intact, candidates to the priesthood need an affective maturity which is prudent, able to renounce anything that is a threat to it, vigilant over both body and spirit, and capable of esteem and respect in interpersonal relationships between men and women. A precious help can be given by a suitable education to true friendship, following the image of the bonds of fraternal affection which Christ himself lived on earth (cf. John 1-1:5) (*ibid.*, n. 45).

The Challenges of Friendship for Celibates

The ability to enter into spiritual friendships requires a certain degree of affective maturity. It also requires a level of spiritual self-discipline. Without constant growth in virtue and the ability to keep one's heart focused on one's primary commitment to Christ, a person's natural tendency toward a holistic expression of love, including those uniquely physical expressions reserved for marriage, will overwhelm one or both friends. This would almost inevitably lead the celibate to compromise his or her life-commitment by occasional or even habitual involvement in sexual sins.

FRIENDSHIP GROWS THROUGH STAGES

Full-blown friendships are almost never formed al at once. "Love at first sight" happens more in Hollywood than anywhere else. Friendship—as a living and creative reality—must grow, and it does so by passing through various stages. It can be helpful to trace the growth of friendship through these stages. We will focus on the "spiritual friendships" of celibates.

Stage 1: Attraction

It all begins with an attraction. This occurs when we feel that mysterious element attracting us to certain people likes or opposites. This stirs us to want to know that person better. Sometimes it is a consciously sensed quality, like strength or beauty, wisdom, or charm, perhaps a sense of humor, or even a sense of holiness that makes us feel some connection with that person. Sometimes it is an unconscious attraction, like being drawn to someone who is a father-figure or a mother-figure, or someone who possesses a quality we wish we could possess, but feel we do not, and so we "possess it" in that individual.

It often happens that many budding friendships never actually develop beyond this initial attraction. This is because either the other person does not respond or he or she actually rejects the possible friendship. All that remains is an unfulfilled attraction.

Genuine friendship (*philia*-love) cannot be forced. It can only be freely given and freely responded to. In this regard, it must be acknowledged that some people are not capable of any depth of *philia*-love because they lack a sufficiently developed "affective maturity." This can cause difficulties for some celibates. Craving this form of love, some celibates try to impose their friendship on others, regardless of whether it is wanted and accepted or not. This imposition merely covers over the loneliness they feel inside instead of satisfying a genuine affective need. Real growth can hardly take place in such a situation.

Furthermore, since such a relationship lacks a basic emotional and spiritual maturity, it frequently degenerates into physical expressions of affection and can easily lead the celibate person into committing sins against chastity, whether with persons of the opposite sex or even of one's own sex. The freedom factor in establishing genuine friendships is a natural safeguard against this danger.

Stage 2: Mutual Bond Established

If the other person does respond to the initial attraction, a real friendship has begun and a mutual bond is now established between the two persons. Once this initial bond is present, the two may seek out each other's company more frequently. They begin to share experiences in which they grow as persons because of the feeling of being mutually accepted, loved, and cared for.

The Danger of Physical (Genital) Desire

It is precisely at this point, as the new friendship is being developed, that a potential danger is met. Friendship involves the mutual response of two fully developed human beings. Being human, we tend to act in a holistic way—with our full physical, emotional and spiritual make-up. Even in a "spiritual friendship," it is natural that the physical as well as the emotional forces within us are drawn into the friendship. This means that we can become desirous of physically expressing the love of our friendship.

There are physical signs of affection proper within celibate friendships. St. Paul, for example, mentions three different times in his writings that the disciples should greet one another with a "holy kiss" (Rom, 16:16; 1 Cor 16:20; 2 Cor 13:12).

However, these are simple forms of affection, and should always be exchanged with respect and discretion. If these signs of affection go beyond the ordinary signs that any Christian can show to any other Christian (something which can be viewed by anyone else without suspicion), there may be an unconscious or even conscious attempt to draw genital sexual pleasure from such actions. These actions might include passionate kissing, improper touches, or any immodesty in appearance, all of which can easily lead to further actions, even to sexual intercourse.

What is needed in regard to physical attraction and the

desire for affectionate expression is the self-discipline of the virtues of chastity and modesty. Chastity controls sexual desire according to the responsibilities of one's state in life, in this case, the celibate state. Celibacy, as we have seen, requires the total renunciation of those actions proper to the physical intimacy of marriage. Self-discipline furthermore requires modesty, controlling the actions of our senses. For example, we must control our eyes against immodest glances, our conversation against suggestive talk, and our touch against improper gestures. Someone entering a spiritual friendship without the self-discipline of acquired virtue will encounter serious temptations and is likely to fall into sins of unchastity.

Not everyone is sufficiently ready to handle the strong physical attraction that can make itself felt, even in faithful and mature spiritual friendshiPs What makes the difference is the ability to reach a certain "detachment" in the friendship, the readiness and joyful willingness to set aside sexual gratification. This is done for the love of Jesus, for the sake of fidelity to one's celibate commitment, out of respect for the integrity of one's friend, and for the sake of preserving deeper, more spiritual satisfactions and blessings which the friendship embodies.

Resisting Emotional Possessiveness

Besides the attraction to physical acts of intimacy, there is a second danger that must be avoided. It is a kind of emotional. possessiveness.[2] Sincere friends are readily aware of the need to avoid any obviously sinful physical expressions of sexual gratification.

However, less obvious is an emotional control that can spring from the friendship. By this kind of possessiveness, one friend may try to dominate or manipulate the other. This may come from an emotional woundedness on the part of one or both partners whose need is for absolute security (i.e., "I have to be sure he/she is my friend"). This engenders a desire to possess or "control" the other person his or her time, attention and preoccupation.

With this possessiveness, one friend tends to want to keep the friend exclusively for oneself. This puts pressure on the partner always to be there for the friend and takes the partner away from his or her duties ("I can't do my work because my friend wants/needs me") and his or her community ("I don't have time for others because my friend always expects me to be with him/her"). This can lead to sins of injustice for example, neglect of duties toward others), of uncharitableness (for example, excluding certain people in the community from due love and service), and even of impiety (for example, deliberate distractions in prayer because of an obsessive preoccupation with one's friend).

Bouts of Jealousy

This possessiveness usually gives rise to intense feelings of jealousy experienced if the friend is seen speaking, working, recreating, studying, or even praying with others. Jealousy usually springs from emotional insecurity; one partner feels threatened when the other is with a third party because of the fear that the third party will "steal away" the exclusive friend. In fact, it usually happens that the greater the insecurity, the greater the possessiveness, exclusiveness, and jealousy!

In marriage, couples have a right to a certain degree of jealousy (but not a limitless controlling or suffocating jealousy) because their marital rights cannot be shared with others. But jealousy has no proper place in spiritual friendships Mature celibate friendships should be characterized by a sense of freedom for each partner.

I once saw a sign that read: "A friend is someone who leaves me with all my freedom intact, but who obliges me to be the best person I can be!" Healthy friendship does not take away a person's freedom; it protects it and encourages it as a creative force for growth and maturation. Such freedom protects friends from the difficulties and dangers of possessiveness, exclusiveness and jealousy which, in the long run, may well destroy the friendship, or at least make it troubled (for example, with bouts of jealousy or conflicts with the legitimate demands of community).

Mutual freedom also helps friends to feel secure and comfortable in exchanging proper signs of affection. It excludes unhealthy displays of sentimentality, such as overly emotional greetings, exaggerated physical embraces, exchanges of sentimental gifts, and the like. Around each person is what might be called a comfort zone. Exaggerated displays of affection intrude into that zone and make the partner feel uncomfortable or "coerced" into affectionate displays he or she would rather avoid. This puts a strain on the friendship because it takes away the partner's freedom of self-expression. Furthermore, certain affections can lead to dangerous sexual arousal and sinful sexual gratification.

Stage 3: Mature Friendship

When these dangers are avoided, the stage is set for the full flowering of celibate friendship in a mutual, free, respectfilled and loving bond. There may still come trials, either between the two friends or caused unjustly by others. Yet, if the friendship is rooted in Jesus' love, it will most likely survive. Occasionally, temptations springing from physical attraction and genital drives will be present; they must be dealt with immediately (without delay) and decisively (without compromise). The counsel of a good spiritual director or confessor can be of enormous help in discerning potential dangers in a friendship and help guard against self-deception.

Friends in Christ

In this fullness of friendship, the friends grow through

their mutual acceptance, love, respect, and encouragement. Talents that were previously either hidden (for fear of rejection) or unknown (they were never brought out by others) now emerge in a new creative, encouraging, and free atmosphere. The key to the stability and growth of celibate friendship on this fullest level is a "Jesus-centeredness." If Jesus is the link that ultimately bonds two together as friends (as were the friendships of the saints), His presence and love assures the spiritual protection and the power to grow in the friendship. They will more carefully avoid the pitfalls on the physical and emotional levels by observing His commandments. Living His love will set them each free in the truth (John 8:32). They will become one in a true bond of *philia*-love, because their love will become one in Jesus' love. Because He says to both of them: "You are my friends" (John 15:14), their friendship will endure forever in His friendship.

Notes

1. The need for "affective maturity" is increasingly stressed in Vatican documents dealing with religious and priestly formation. *Directives*, for example, when listing the requirements of Church law for a candidate to be admitted into the novitiate, mentions: "A balanced affectivity, especially sexual balance, which presupposes the acceptance of the other, man or woman, respecting his or her own difference" (n. 43). It also lists "the ability to live in community," since this demands a maturity in emotional expression and control (*ibid.*).

Another document, *Fraternal Life in Community*, issued by the Congregation for Institutes of Consecrated Life and Societies of Apostolic Life, and approved by Pope John Paul II on January 15, 1994, emphasizes this point:

Fraternal life in common requires from all members good psychological balance within which each individual can achieve emotional maturity. . . . One essential element of such growth is emotional freedom, which enables consecrated persons to love their vocation and to love in accordance with this vocation. It is precisely this freedom and this maturity which allow us to live out our affectivity correctly, both inside and outside the community.

To love one's vocation, to hear the call as something that gives true meaning to life, and to cherish consecration as a true, beautiful, and good reality which gives truth, beauty and goodness to one's own existence, all of this makes a person strong and autonomous, secure in one's own identity, free of the need for various forms of support and compensation, especially in the area of affectivity. All this reinforces the bond that links the consecrated person to those who share his or her calling. It is with them, first and foremost, that he or she feels called to live relationships of fraternity and friendship.

To love one's vocation is to love the Church, it is to love one's institute, and to experience the community as one's own family.

To love in accordance with one's vocation is to love in the manner of one who, in every human relationship, wishes to be a clear sign of the love of God, not invading and not possessing, but loving and desiring the good of the other with God's own benevolence.

Therefore, special formation is required in the area of affectivity to promote an integration of the human aspect with the more specifcally spiritual aspect (n. 37).

2. *Directives* cautions against the self-centeredness that can give rise to emotional possessiveness as well as acts of sexual gratification. The antidote is found in humility and

genuine concern for others.

An instinctive tendency of the human person leads to making an absolute out of human love. It is a tendency characterized by self-centeredness, which asserts itself through a domination over the person loved as if happiness could be secured from this possession. On the other hand, one finds it very difficult to understand and especially to realize that love can be lived in a total dedication of oneself, without necessarily requiring a sexual manifestation of it. Education for chastity will therefore aim at helping each one to control and to master his or her sexual impulses, while at the same time, it will avoid a self-centeredness that is content with one's fidelity to purity. It is no accident that the ancient Fathers [of the Church] gave priority to humility over chastity, since this latter can be accompanied, as experience has shown, by a hardness of heart (n.1-3).

CHAPTER 12

Growing in Celibate Love

Celibate love, like all love, can and must grow. It follows the same laws that apply to the spiritual life in general. There is an old saying that: "If we are not going forward in the spiritual life, we are going backward!" Those who are earnestly trying to live their celibate commitment can, generally assume that by the very fact that they have persevered in it, they are growing in celibate love. At the same time, the teachings of our Lord provide certain means to help this growth in the virtue of chastity. They can be divided between "spiritual means" and "practical means."

SPIRITUAL MEANS

Prayer

One of the first and most important means to grow in celibate love is prayer. Through prayer we ask and obtain grace from God. Since grace is needed to grow in love, prayer strengthens and preserves our commitment to celibate love. The Servant of God Archbishop Sheen outlined the following steps by which a priest or religious could fall away from their celibate vocation:

1. Neglect of prayer;
2. Pulling away to a distance from Jesus in the Eucharist;
3. Giving one's self over to a comfortable life;
4. Carelessness or neglect regarding the occasions of sin;
5: Substitution of a creature for Christ.

From these steps, it is obvious that prayer is the celibate's primary and vital link to Christ. Thus, frequent, daily contact with God through prayer sustains every aspect of our Christian life. Prayer is what gives vitality to faith, charity, the spirit of sacrifice, and also to one's celibacy.

Two links between prayer and celibacy are worth noting. First, celibacy makes prayer more necessary. This is due to the fact that by renouncing the intimacy or companionship of marriage the celibate must fill the resulting "void" with a deeper relationship with Christ. This goes back to St. Paul's teaching that the heart of the celibate must be "undivided," focused on Christ as the center of its love and source of its strength.

Second, celibacy allows those persons vowed to celibacy to have more time for prayer. Without the cares and preoccupations of married and family life, celibate persons are freer to focus more time, attention, and energy on their relationship with Christ. As a retreat director once said: "If you are celibate and you do not pray, you are wasting your time." Prayer should be an essential characteristic of the life of every celibate person, whether a priest, religious, or lay person.

The Eucharist

Following from prayer is devotion to Jesus in the Eucharist. This devotion provides a sense of "warmth," something which helps celibates deal with the loneliness they will experience from time to time. By fostering a deep personal love for Jesus in the Eucharist, they receive grace and strength, leading to a deepened sense of personal friendship with Jesus which helps sustain them in life.

Mass, when possible on a daily basis, should be their central focus. From the Holy Sacrifice of the Mass, they will draw the graces and courage to meet the challenges of the day. Receiving Christ in Holy Communion, they renew their relationship to the Lord and their awareness of His intimate presence in their lives.

A Eucharist-centered piety should emphasize prayer before Jesus in the Blessed Sacrament. Accordingly, eucharistic adoration should play an important role in their spiritual lives. Celibates consecrated to God, especially in the priesthood and religious life, should take as a guide the words of our Lord to the apostles in the Garden of Gethsemane: "Could you not watch and pray one hour with Me?" A daily Holy Hour can be a source of enormous spiritual strength and daily renewal.[1]

Other Devotions to our Lord

Devotion to our Lord can take many forms. Two that are especially important are devotion to His Passion and to His Sacred Heart. Prayerful reflection on the Passion of Christ can stir up a generous love within us. This love, in turn, will move us to make the sacrifices involved in celibate living as well as strengthen us to overcome temptations, even severe ones, against chastity. St. Paul could say that the love of Christ urges us on (cf. 2 Cor 5:14). Seeing what Christ has suffered moves us to want to return our love to Him for the love He has shown us.

This response of our love to Jesus' love is also true of devotion to His Sacred Heart. Since the Sacred Heart of Jesus represents His unqualified love for us, devotion to His Sacred Heart is really directed at His total love for us. When we focus on the Heart of Jesus, we are moved to recognize how deeply

He loved each one of us. Because of the love that He felt for us, Jesus gave His life for us on the Cross. Now we must return that love. St. Francis of Assisi used to say: "Greatly to be loved is the love of Him who has loved us so much!" Our love for Him helps us desire and determine to remain faithful to Him.

Frequent Confession

Confession is a powerful means to sustain one's commitment to Christ and to the Church. Confession gives us first and foremost the forgiveness of our sins, freeing us from guilt for the wrongs we have done. Confession removes sin from our hearts and gives us the opportunity to begin again to show our love for our Lord and for others.

In addition to the forgiveness of sins, we also receive through the Sacrament of Reconciliation the right to those "sacramental graces" needed to overcome sin in the future and to reform our lives. These are called "sacramental graces" because they assist us in achieving the purpose of the sacrament (the forgiveness of past and present sins, and the reform of our lives so as to avoid sin in the future). Sacramental grace will certainly strengthen us in our daily resolve to live chastely.

Peace

Along with forgiveness, through the Sacrament of Reconciliation, we also experience the peace of Christ. On Easter night, our Risen Lord bestowed on the apostles His gift of peace along with the power to forgive sins. He linked them in a special way because the forgiveness of sins would be one of the greatest sources of peace: "Jesus said to them again, 'Peace be with you' . . . He breathed on them, and said to them, 'Receive the Holy Spirit. If you forgive the sins of any, they are forgiven'" (John 20:21-23).

St. Paul describes two qualities of this peace of Christ (cf. Phil 4:7). First, he tells us it is beyond all human understanding.

This is because it is the peace of Christ and not the peace of the world. Only someone rooted in Christ through faith and love can begin to comprehend the reality of His peace.

A second quality of the peace of Christ is that it will stand guard over our hearts and minds and keep them focused on Christ. Persons gifted with the peace of Christ find themselves less restless, more intent on the Lord and on spiritual things, and less distracted by the passing allurements and attractions of the world and the flesh. This peace is a gift beyond measure for anyone living a Christian life, especially those embracing celibacy.

Joy

Along with the peace that comes from the Sacrament of Reconciliation is the gift of joy. Like peace (cf. John 14:27), Jesus promised His joy to His disciples at the Last Supper (cf. John 15:11). Joy, a gift of Jesus and one of the fruits of the Holy Spirit working in us (cf. Gal 5:22), can be a powerful antidote to temptations against chastity.

Anyone familiar with Alcoholics Anonymous knows there are difficult times for a person with alcoholic tendencies, times when they are more likely to be tempted to indulge themselves. They usually express these times with the acronym HALT, which stands for hungry, angry, lonely, tired.

The same is true for a person practicing chastity, especially a celibate. Times of depression, self-pity and morbid curiosity easily bring on feelings of general sexual restlessness or arousal and are, therefore, spiritually dangerous. To counteract these, the Lord gives us His joy which lifts our spirits, thereby countering the downward pull of depression and self-pity. This joy makes celibates eager for good and not for evil, and gives a feeling of delight in goodness which counters the allurement of sensual pleasure.

St. Francis was keenly aware of the importance of

spiritual joy. He would say: "The devil rejoices most when he can steal the joy out of the heart of the servant of God." On other occasions, he put it this way: "The devil cannot harm the servant of God whom he sees filled with holy joy!" This joy is one of the benefits of frequent confession and a great spiritual protection for celibacy.

Spiritual Counsel

Confession can also provide the opportunity for helpful counsel and advice. This can be especially important for persons who feel that their trials or difficulties in living celibacy are worse than they really are. St. Francis de Sales wisely cautioned that we must not mistake the rustling of leaves for the clashing of swords. Anyone who only heard the noise but could not see what was causing it might easily mistake rustling leaves for clashing swords. Needless to say, they are vastly different! In a similar way, we often lack a clear view of our own problems. Other people often can have a better perspective on our situation than we do. Being honest and humble in Confession about difficulties with problems related to celibacy can be a "graced moment" in which God helps to deliver us from such trials, especially from the deceit of the devil. The devil is always seeking not only to lead people into sin but also into discouragement so that they will abandon their celibate vocation. Good advice in the confessional not only unmasks the devil's deceits, but it usually dispels fears, anxieties, and confusion as well.

REGULAR SPIRITUAL DIRECTION

In addition to Confession, celibates, especially those who go on to the priesthood or religious life, generally need the help of regular spiritual direction. A spiritual director is not only for advice and counsel, but also to help us understand how the Holy Spirit is leading us in the spiritual life. Good spiritual directors possess understanding of the spiritual life, prudent judgment, common sense, and a certain element of kindness in dealing with those they direct. They are willing to let the Holy Spirit lead the person, and not simply impose their own agenda on the directee.

Those who are discerning a call to celibacy would do well to speak about their feelings with a spiritual director. Besides dealing with the questions, fears and hesitations that often plague young people considering celibacy, good spiritual direction (as well as good initial formation in a seminary or convent) can help them to integrate their lives in terms of where they are coming from and where they are headed.[2] It goes without saying that the direction given should be based on solid Catholic teaching and on firm principles of spiritual theology.

Many persons consecrated to celibacy feel a need for regular spiritual direction. The frequency of direction can vary (for example, from once a month to once every two or three months or longer) and is usually determined by the needs of the individual being directed and the time and availability of the director.

Devotion to Our Lady

Devotion to the Blessed Virgin Mary is especially powerful in regard to chastity. The Servant of God Archbishop Fulton J. Sheen used to say: "When devotion to Mary is strong, there is a deeper appreciation for virginity, motherhood and marital fidelity." This is because Mary is an outstanding example of these three aspects of Christian life. It seems that our Blessed Lady has been given a special power of intercession for those who are committed to celibate living. Celibates must frequently turn to her, not only as an example, but also as an intercessor for the graces they need to live their commitment faithfully.

There are two prayer devotions to Our Lady that are highly recommended in connection with chastity. The first of these is the Rosary. Papal statements, examples from Church history, and the experience of countless individuals all bear witness to the fact of Mary's powerful intercession through the Rosary. Padre Pio, the sainted Capuchin Franciscan priest who had the stigmata (or five wounds of Christ) used to say of the Rosary: "Is there a prayer more beautiful or more pleasing than the one she taught us herself? More beautiful than the Rosary? Always say the Rosary!" Daily or at least frequent recitation of the Rosary is a very effective means of protecting and preserving chastity, the foundation of the celibate commitment.

A second devotion to Our Lady recommended by many of the saints is that of saying the "Three Hail Mary's." This devotion consists of praying three Hail Mary's every morning and every night while consecrating our mind (thoughts and desires), our heart (affections), and our body (actions) to our Lady's care, seeking her protection from all mortal sins, especially those against chastity. Persons who faithfully practice this devotion usually find it to be a powerful means of safeguarding their celibate consecration.

PRACTICAL MEANS TO CELIBACY

Support of Christian Community

Because celibates lack the intimacy and companionship proper to marriage, they must find some degree of human support through their association with fellow Christians. This is important because it provides a human touch of warmth, caring, and affirmation. For religious, much of this human support has traditionally been found in their relationships with members of their own particular community. Warmth in community life can be a tremendous antidote to temptations of loneliness, self-pity, and ultimately any behavior contrary to chastity.

Fraternal support also includes sharing one's concerns, needs and difficulties. St. Francis, for example, mentions in his

Rule of 1223 that wherever the friars happen to be and meet one another, they should feel confident to make known to each other their needs and concerns.[3] These may be obvious physical needs which are generally easier to fulfill, At other times, they may be spiritual in nature. These latter can be alleviated in some measure by the assistance and advice of others in a fraternal-spirit.

Furthermore, a warm, caring community can be a healing place when members are suffering, a supportive place when members experience their own personal weakness, in a word, a place where the compassionate but challenging love of Jesus is experienced through one's brothers and sisters in Christ.[4]

For those who live in a greater degree of isolation, for example, diocesan priests, the support of other priests in their locality is an enormous help. It is important that they have close priest friends as well as "support groups" of fellow priests with whom they can get together for prayer, mutual discussion of problems, and relaxation.

There is also a need to cultivate friendships with lay persons, including those with whom they work. (This -last point highlights again the importance of mutual affirmation, respect, and support between celibates, especially priests or religious, and the laity.)

The Need for Self-Discipline

Chastity is not possible without a spirit of sacrifice and self-denial. This requires that the celibate be grounded in a healthy sense of self-discipline.[5] On one occasion Christ drove an "unclean spirit" (a demon of lust?) out of a young man. The apostles had not been able to drive this same "unclean spirit" out of the young man. Afterward, they asked our Lord why they could not drive it out. Jesus answered them: "This kind does not leave but by prayer and fasting" (Matt 17:21). Fasting, added to the power of prayer, gives strength to drive away temptations and any demonic spirit of lust. This teaching of our Lord has been reinforced by the long experience of the Church in her individual members.

Discretion in the Use of Media

There is an old, wise saying: "Prudence is the better part of valor." It means that in life, using our common sense and good judgment, we can avoid unnecessary conflicts as well as difficulties that might otherwise overwhelm the strength we think we have. Applied to living celibacy faithfully, it means avoiding unnecessary and potentially harmful temptations by avoiding viewing any material aimed at arousing sexual pleasure and desires. After all, our Lord Himself taught us to ask our Heavenly Father: "Lead us not into temptation, but deliver us from evil." This is especially important today because of society's attitude of extreme sexual permissiveness. This is manifested in an increasing degree of explicit pornographic material being presented by all forms of the media.

This is an important area of concern for all Christians, but especially for priests and religious.[6] Much harm has been done to the spiritual lives of many people because of a lack of control over curiosity about sexual matters. Sometimes this curiosity, if not properly dealt with, becomes an obsessive-compulsive need. If no real discretion is exercised in the use of media, it is difficult to see how any significant growth in living chastely, much less joyfully and cheerfully, can be made.

Avoid Idleness

How true it is that "idleness is the devil's workshop." When persons are idle, they can become slothful, spiritually lazy, or excessively curious. Idleness can expose the person to many needless temptations. Genuine work can be healthy, not only for the body but also for the soul. It absorbs attention, thus lessening the danger of idle daydreaming and curiosity.

Furthermore, when persons find satisfaction in their work, whether it be manual or intellectual, there is a certain fulfillment that comes with that work. St. Francis of Assisi was very insistent on the need for honest work to be done by his friars, not only to give good example to the people and to support themselves, but also to avoid the danger of idleness, which he called "the enemy of the soul."

A word of caution, however, can be useful regarding the very opposite of "idleness," and that is "workaholism." This is when a person simply plunges into activities of all kinds just to be busy for "busyness'" sake. Workaholism differs from being genuinely busy, the result of many necessary things to be done. Workaholism has a compulsive quality to it, a driven need, possibly to avoid dealing directly with something else.

Workaholism can pose a danger to celibate living in two ways. First, it can easily be a form of escape or of drowning out one's problems and depression by keeping busy. The danger here is not dealing with the root causes of one's problems, especially of any sexual difficulties. Though they are "out of sight" temporarily, such problems, if not addressed, tend to fester subconsciously and usually re-emerge more forcefully in the future.

A second potential danger to celibacy is that workaholism often ends up exhausting the person physically (from lack of proper sleep and eating habits, or by sheer overwork) and spiritually (by neglect of prayer). This can result in a person's moral and physical resistance being impaired, leaving them more susceptible to various sexual temptations. A sense of balance and moderation has been lost from a person's life and must be restored; the Christian ideal is "a sound mind in a sound body."

Directives states the following as help for living consecrated chastity: "an appreciation of the body and its proper functioning, and the acquiring of an elementary physical hygiene, including adequate sleep, exercise, relaxation, nourishment, and the like" (n. 13).

OVERCOME PRIDE AND HARDNESS OF HEART

St. Thomas Aquinas taught that when a person has strong pride, God sometimes will permit sexual trials and even sexual sins in order to humble them and thereby break their pride. He argued that pride is a worse sin than unchastity, but that unchastity is more shameful. God uses the humiliation of these trials and even the failures of sexual sins to tear down pride in the hearts of people when that pride cannot be removed in any other way. These difficulties and sins move these individuals to seek God's mercy and help with humble and contrite hearts. It follows that if a person humbles himself or herself, then God will not have to humble that person. In fact, though God resists the proud, He generously gives His grace to the humble (cf. 1 Pet 5:5).

At the same time, no one can live a celibate life without the mercy of God. If a person wants to win the mercy of God—and celibates need that grace of mercy to live their life of sacrifice—then they must give mercy to others. God bestows His mercy on those who bestow mercy on others. Our Lord said clearly:

> "Judge not, and you will not be judged; condemn not, and you will not be condemned; forgive, and you will be forgiven; give, and it will be given to you. . . . For the measure you give will be the measure you get back." (Luke 5:37-38)

Therefore, an attitude of kindness, gentleness, and a nonjudgmental (non-condemning) spirit will win God's favor, grace, and mercy, enabling the celibate person to live in greater fidelity. He or she will experience—through the merciful hand of God—the joy, peace, and love that results from a celibate commitment lived to the full.

Notes

1. Archbishop Sheen recommended a daily Holy Hour before the Blessed Sacrament for all priests, religious, and lay persons (the latter when possible).

Bl. Mother Teresa of Kolkata once gave this advice to a priest who asked her what is needed to be a good priest: "Make your Holy Hour faithfully before the Blessed Sacrament each day, and never deliberately do anything you know offends God, and you will be a good priest."

2. *Directives* mentions as a goal of religious formation that of "Helping each [candidate] to profit by past personal experiences, whether positive, in order to give thanks for them, or negative, in order to be aware of one's weaknesses, in order to humble oneself peacefully before God and to remain vigilant for the future" (n.13).

3. St. Francis wrote in his Rule of 1223:

"And wherever the brothers may be together or meet [other] brothers, let them give witness that they are members of one family. And let each one confidently make known his need to the other, for if a mother has such care and love for her son born according to the flesh, should not someone love and care for his brother according to the Spirit even more diligently" (Ch. 6)?

4. The document *Fraternal Life in Community* states:

Difficulties in this area [of affectivity and sexuality] ... can be a result of difficulties in community or apostolate. A rich and warm fraternal life, one that "carries the burden" of the wounded brother or sister in need of help, is thus particularly important.

While a certain maturity is necessary for life in community, a cordial fraternal life is equally necessary in order to allow each religious to attain maturity.

Where members of a community become aware of diminished affective autonomy in one of their brothers or sisters, the response on the part of the community ought to be one of rich and human love, similar to that of our Lord Jesus and of many holy religious—a love that shares in fears and joys, difficulties and hopes, with that warmth that is particular to a new heart that knows how to accept the whole person. Such love—caring and respectful, gratuitous rather than possessive—should make the love of our Lord seem very near: that love which caused the Son of God to proclaim through the Cross that we cannot doubt that we are loved by Love. (n. 37)

5. The *CCC* presents self-discipline as "a training in human freedom:"

Chastity includes an *apprenticeship in self-mastery* which is a training in human freedom. The alternative is clear: either man governs his passions and finds peace, or he lets himself be dominated by them and becomes unhappy. "Man's dignity therefore requires him to act out of conscious and free choice, as moved and drawn in a personal way from within, and not by blind impulses in himself or by mere external constraint. Man gains such dignity when, ridding himself of all slavery to the passions, he presses forward to his goal by freely choosing what is good and, by his diligence and skill, effectively secures for himself the means suited to this end" (n. 2339).

Directives also lists among the goals for formation in consecrated chastity the need to provide assistance "in matters of self-control on the sexual and affective level, but also with respect to other instinctive or acquired needs (sweets, tobacco, alcohol)" (n. 13).

6. The *Directory for the Life and Ministry of Priests*

gives a practical caution to priests, and what it says can apply just as profitably to all celibates:

> It is clear that in order to guarantee and protect this gift [of chastity in celibacy] in a climate of serenity and spiritual progress, possible difficulties for the priests should be avoided by use of appropriate measures... Priests, then, must not fail to follow those ascetical norms which are proven by the Church's experience and which are demanded even more in present-day circumstances. In this way they may prudently avoid frequenting places, attending shows or reading materials which constitute a danger to the observance of celibate chastity. In making use of means of social communication, whether as pastoral aids or for leisure, they must observe the necessary discretion and avoid anything which could harm their vocation (n. 60).

CHAPTER 13

The Fruits of Celibate Love

A favorite image in Sacred Scripture for the Christian life is to compare it to the work of a farmer who sows seeds in his field, cares for his crops, and gathers in a harvest. In one parable our Lord compares the kingdom of heaven to a farmer who goes out sowing good seed which bears or fails to bear fruit according to the soil in which it is planted (Matt 13:4-23). In another parable, He compares the kingdom to a field where good wheat has been sown by a farmer (symbol for God) while an enemy (symbol for the devil) sows weeds. The wheat represents those who authentically respond to the gospel message and live good Christian lives; the weeds represent those who reject the message of Christ in their own lives and even try to oppose the work of the Church. At harvest time, the wheat will be gathered into the farmer's barn (i.e., joy in God's kingdom) while the weeds will be burned (i.e., sorrow and eternal punishment) (cf. Matt 13:24-30, 36-43). Our Lord even adds a third parable about a mustard seed—proverbial for the smallest quantity or amount of something—that grows into a large shrub. The message is that the kingdom, despite its small beginning, will have enormous growth (cf. Matt 13:31-32).

St. Paul picks up this same theme when he writes: "He

who sows sparingly will also reap sparingly, and he who sows bountifully will also reap bountifully" (2 Cor 9:6).

SPIRITUAL HARVEST

The harvest, from its first fruits to its final full crop, is the only thing that really matters.[1] All the labor of sowing, watering, fertilizing, and weeding is useless if there is no harvest. Excluding natural catastrophes, such as drought or pestilence, if the plants sown are given proper care, they will bear their appropriate fruit. In a similar manner, if a Christian lives his or her life of faith in Christ, giving it the proper care (for example, prayer, the Eucharist, Reconciliation) and avoiding those factors which destroy that life (sin and its occasions), then he or she will bear a spiritual harvest.

Celibacy has certain "fruits" or effects that it unfailingly produces as long as the person lives it in love and freedom. This is the goal of the celibate's life, for our Heavenly Father is glorified in our bearing "much fruit" (John 15:8), producing an abundance of good deeds.

It is possible to be celibate, however, and not bear authentic or desirable fruit. This is reflected in the Gospel parable about the ten bridesmaids (cf. Matt 25:1-13). All ten bridesmaids were virgins. Therefore, they were all chaste and celibate. However, Our Lord says that only five of them were sensible because they took oil along with them (which St. Augustine says was the oil of charity). The other five virgins were foolish, because they did not provide any oil (charity) for their lamps The meaning here is that if celibacy makes a person bitter, resentful, cold-hearted—in other words, lacking charity both for God and neighbor—it would profit him or her nothing. (It was said of the Jansenist nuns of Port Royal in France: "They were as pure as angels, but as proud as devils!") If a celibate person is proud or disdaining toward others, and there is total lack of the oil of charity, then celibacy does not produce the desired fruit nor does it help on the road to salvation and sanctification.

On the other hand, our Lord tells us that a good tree must bear good fruit (cf. Matt 7:16-20). Our Lord says that you can tell a tree by its fruit; good fruit indicates a sound tree. This is seen in the practice of virtue which can only authentically come from God. It produces the effects of peace and encouragement, both in the individual who practices celibacy and in those whose lives he or she affects. On the other hand, if the fruit is bad, this indicates a decayed tree. This is known as a pseudo-virtue[2] which springs from self-love or from the devil. Such pseudo-virtue would ultimately cause spiritual hardship, confusion, and scandal. In short, we may conclude that if celibacy is the authentic work of God's grace in us, it must bear authentic and good fruit.

THE GOOD FRUITS OF AUTHENTIC CELIBACY

When celibates are sustained in their commitment by the grace of the Holy Spirit, they will bear the good fruits of celibacy.

A Union of "Spousal Love" with Christ and the Church

By Baptism, all Christians are united with Christ through Sanctifying Grace; we become living members of Christ (cf. 1 Cor 6:15, 12:27). However, through celibacy freely chosen for the sake of the kingdom of God, we become more uniquely joined to Christ and His Church. This is an aspect of union called "spousal love." First of all, it foreshadows the spiritual union all the saints have with Jesus in heaven where all the saints are celibate.[3] Jesus is the Divine Bridegroom; the Church, made up of all the saints, is His "Bride." He loves the Church and cares for His saints (on earth as well as in heaven) in terms of a groom loving and caring for his bride, and the Church relates in return as a bride loving and caring for her groom. St. Paul writes of this glorious yet mysterious "spousal relationship" in his letter to the Christians at Ephesus:

> Husbands, love your wives as Christ loved the Church and gave Himself up for her, that He might sanctify her, having cleansed her by the washing of water with the word, that He might present the Church to Himself in splendor, without spot or wrinkle or any such thing, that she might be holy and without blemish. This mystery is a profound one, and I am saying that it refers to Christ and the Church (Eph 5:24-27, 32).

The celibate, with an "undivided heart"—with no earthly spouse to share this love with—focuses the whole of his or her unique love on Jesus alone. The individual celibate, whether man or woman, seeks to grow in this union with Jesus, which images the union of husband and wife.[4]

As an overflow of "spousal love" for Jesus, the celibate consecrated for the sake of the kingdom of heaven is caught up into Jesus' "spousal love" for His Church. This is especially true of clerical celibacy. Jesus' relationship to His Church as Groom to Bride is essentially part of His priestly mission wherein He offers himself out of "spousal love" to sanctify and cleanse the Church, so she might be holy, a "spotless Bride" (Rev 21:2). By his ordination, a priest shares in Jesus' priesthood and therefore also in Jesus' "spousal love" for the Church. This means that a priest has a new relationship of "spousal love" to the Church and, like Christ, he must work to sanctify the Church by his priestly ministry. His celibate status, free of an earthly spouse, allows him uniquely to fulfill his "spousal love" for the Church.[5] what is true of a priest is even more applicable to, a bishop.[6] It should be noted that the relationship of "spousal love" applies also to the consecrated celibacy of religious in a special way.[7]

Fosters Greater Dependence on the Lord

Celibate persons clearly recognize their spiritual frailty and weakness. St. Augustine once prayed: "Lord, let me distrust myself and trust in you!" This prayer reflects the sentiments that our Lord told the apostles at the Last Supper, namely, that without Him, they could do nothing (cf. John 15:5). St. Paul, in one of his letters, says that we carry a treasure but in an earthen vessel (cf. 2 Cor 4:7). Speaking on one occasion to a gathering of priests, Pope John Paul II quoted St. Paul and reminded the priests that the "treasure" they carry was their priesthood. I often think of celibacy as an important part of that fragile earthen vessel which sustains the treasure of the priesthood within it. It demands God's constant grace and strength to keep it intact!

This clear recognition of dependence on the Lord causes the celibate person to be extra vigilant in the service of God, avoiding those things that would hinder his or her celibate commitment. He or she should certainly heed the words our Lord spoke to the three apostles in the Garden of Gethsemane, that they should watch and pray with Him. The importance of prayer in the life of a celibate has already been stressed. But the celibate also needs to be "watchful," avoiding those things that we call "occasions of sin" (persons, places, or things that tend to lead a person into sin), recognizing one's weakness, and knowing that strength will come only from Christ.

SENSITIVITY TO HUMAN WEAKNESS

When celibates recognize their own weakness and need for continuous grace and mercy from God, they gradually become careful not to condemn others in a harsh or critical manner. Sensitive to their own weaknesses, they become increasingly sensitive to others in their human weaknesses, especially those of the flesh. Our Lord said that the spirit was willing but the flesh (human nature) was weak (cf. Mark 14:38). In the case of priests especially, their celibacy can make them mindful of a very significant part of their priestly service:

> For every high priest chosen from among men is appointed to act on behalf of men in relation to God, to offer gifts and sacrifices for sins. He can deal gently with the ignorant and wayward, since he himself is beset with weakness. Because of this he is bound to offer sacrifice for his own sins as well as for those of the people (Heb 5:1-3).

FREE TO BE OF SERVICE

Celibacy frees those who embrace it to be ready to go wherever they are needed. This important aspect of celibacy was brought home to me some years ago when I was teaching in a high school seminary. The seminary faculty and student body held an ecumenical gathering for non-Catholic clergy in our local area. At a dinner we held for the clergy, I sat between two Protestant ministers, both of whom were married. I asked each of them, in turn, how their marriage affected their ministry. The first minister told me he and his wife made an agreement when they got married: So much time would be given for family and so much time would be given for the church. There was a boundary line, and it was not to be crossed. I have to imagine that, at times, this must have caused a certain tension.[8] The second minister said to me: "I feel that I am married twice— to my wife and to my church!" He obviously experienced the tension of the "divided heart," being drawn in two different directions.

GREAT SPIRITUAL FRUITFULNESS

The history of the Church as well as the experience of individuals provide ample evidence that when the celibate life is lived faithfully it becomes a source of spiritual fruitfulness in the Church.

St. Augustine alluded to this in his interpretation of the three degrees of harvest that our Lord mentions in the parable of the Sower and the seed harvests of thirty-fold, sixty-fold and one hundred-fold. Augustine understood these numbers to be symbolic. For him, the one hundred-fold were the martyrs, for it was believed from the earliest Christian times that the blood of the martyrs is the seed of the Church. Wherever martyrs shed their blood for Christ, the Church experiences a renewal of Christian life.

St. Augustine saw the thirty-fold as the ordinary devout Christians who lived good lives, thus bearing fruit for the kingdom.

Finally, he saw the sixty-fold as those who were dedicated to celibacy, namely, virgins, monks and the like. They partook of some of the intensity of spiritual fruitfulness which was characteristic of the martyrs, over and above the ordinary Christian life.

In an earlier chapter, the spiritual maternity of the Blessed Virgin Mary was mentioned.[9] She is the exemplar par excellence of everyone who, committed-to perpetual celibacy, could yet bring forth new life. It was her privilege to give flesh to Jesus. In a somewhat similar manner, those who are committed to celibacy, though having no "physical children" of their own, help to bring forth "spiritual children" for the kingdom. St. Paul was very conscious of this. He told some of his disciples, that though they may have had many guardians (teachers) in Christ, he was their only father in Christ, who begot them through the preaching of the Gospel (cf. 1 Cor 4:15).

The spiritual fruitfulness of celibacy can be understood in the following way: As celibate persons struggle against temptations of lust that would offend chaste celibacy, they merit many graces. These graces are then applied not only for the individual celibate's own needs, but also for those whose lives are caught up in sins of unchastity. These celibates often merit the grace of conversion for someone who would otherwise be lost. At Fatima, Our Lady told Lucia, one of the young visionaries there: "Many souls are lost from God because there is no one to pray and sacrifice for them!", The prayers and sacrifices of those struggling to remain faithful to celibacy are very effective in winning the grace of conversion for others, especially for those who sin against chastity.

St. Paul said that in the sufferings in his own body, he made up what was lacking in the sufferings of Christ for the sake of His Body, the Church (cf. Col 1:24). St. Paul was conscious that his own struggles and sufferings of all kinds would be beneficial, not only for his own growth in holiness, but also for the conversion and growth in holiness of others.

Because there is a union of one member in the Mystical Body with all the other members through union with Christ our Head and in the Holy Spirit, each member of the Mystical Body of Christ can affect the others. St. Paul said that if one member is healthy, all the other members are made healthier, sharing in the health of that one member.

At the same time, however, if one member is ill or fails to remain faithful, their illness will affect other members of the Mystical Body (cf. 1 Cor 12:20). This can happen when those committed to celibacy are not faithful. Not only will grace not be there for others, but many times scandals and other sins lead people astray from true moral living and ultimately away from God and the Church.

The saintly Curé of Ars, St. John Vianney, who would hear confessions for up to fifteen hours a day, once made this statement: "Were it not for a few chaste souls, God would long ago have punished the world." It is the presence of those faithfully committed to celibacy who help to maintain a spirit of true Christian morality and life in the world. This gives to celibacy a certain efficacy or power to transform and renew not only the Church, but also the very society we live in, a society so prone to seeking sexual pleasure in an irresponsible way.

Chastity frees the human heart in a remarkable manner (1 Cor 7:32-35), so that it burns with a love for God and for all people. One of the greatest contributions which religious can bring to humanity today is certainly that of revealing, by their life more than by their words, the possibility of a true dedication to and openness toward others, in sharing their joys, in being faithful and constant in love without a thought of domination or exclusiveness (*Directives*, n. 13).

The celibate man or woman, by his or her commitment, proclaims to the world that people cannot live only for the passing pleasures of the flesh, but must seek those rewards and joys that God has prepared for those who love Him. Celibacy, then, becomes truly a sign of the life we will live in the kingdom of heaven with Christ forever and ever.

PERSEVERANCE THROUGH HOPE

In the Christian life, perseverance is very important. Our Lord tells us that those who persevere till the end will be saved (cf. Matt 24:13). This is especially important regarding celibacy. Whether persons are already committed to celibacy by their vows or are presently discerning such a commitment, perseverance is necessary. Even if, because of human weakness and the allurements of temptation, a person falls into sins against chastity, it is important to get up again and to continue the journey. If it is a matter of discouragement because of intense struggles, St. James reminds us that if we resist these temptations long enough, they will eventually leave us, at least for a time (cf. Jas 4:7).

In these situations, we need the motivation of hope, especially a hope for the rewards the Lord has promised those who love and serve Him faithfully. After all, He will not forget the love we have for Him, and the good we have tried to do for Him and for His people (cf. Heb 6:10). Furthermore, He is faithful. St. Paul assures us that if God has begun a good work in us here, the work of living our celibacy, He will bring that work to completion in our lives (cf. Phil 1:6).

Realizing the importance of hope, St. Francis often challenged his followers to be faithful to their commitment by reminding them of the rewards that await them for faithful service:

Great things have we promised to God,
but greater things has He promised to us.
Let us observe the former,
and earnestly aspire to the latter.
Sensual pleasure is brief,
but everlasting is the punishment.
Short is the suffering,
but eternal is the glory.
Everyone shall be rewarded
according to their merit.

Notes

1. To paraphrase the late, great football coach of the Green Bay Packers Vince Lombardi: "Winning isn't everything; it's the only thing!" Christians could say: "Our salvation isn't everything, it's the only thing!"

2. By "pseudo-virtue," I mean that which appears to be authentic virtue produced by God's grace but which is only an outward appearance of virtue; it lacks any inner reality.

3. Jesus tells us in the Gospel that in heaven everyone will be celibate, for He says: "At the resurrection, they neither marry nor are given in marriage but are like the angels in Heaven"

(Matt 22:30).

Celibacy lived here and now on earth is a foreshadowing of the life of heaven where each of us will find our fulfillment in spiritual union with God. *Directives* calls celibacy assumed for the sake of the kingdom of heaven "a sign of the future world" (n.13). This is often referred to as the "eschatological" sign-value of celibacy, which comes from the Greek word *eschata*, meaning, the "last things," namely, death, judgment, heaven or hell. Celibacy is a preview, however obscure, of this aspect of the life of the saints in heaven!

4. The soul has no gender quality, so every soul, whether of a man or of a woman, relates to Jesus as the one who fulfills it. Obviously, women would tend to speak more freely in terms of relating to Jesus as spouse, but mystically, every soul is said to relate to Him in precisely this manner since union with the Divine Bridegroom is spiritual.

5. This is why the Latin Church has always maintained the practice of priestly celibacy and insists that it rests on profound theological and pastoral motives. The *Directory for the Life and Ministry of Priests* comments on this relationship in connection with the "spousal love" of Christ and the Church:

> To live with love and generosity the gift received (of consecrated celibacy), it is particularly important that the priest understand from the beginning of his seminary formation the theological and spiritual motives of ecclesiastical discipline on celibacy. This particular gift of God demands the observance of chastity, the perfect and perpetual continence for the kingdom of heaven, so sacred ministers can more easily adhere to Christ with an undivided heart and dedicate themselves more freely to the service of God and man. The ecclesiastical discipline ... finds its ultimate reason in the intimate bond which celibacy has with holy ordination, which shapes the priest to Jesus Christ,

Head and Spouse of the Church.

The Letter to the Ephesians (cf. 5:25-27) shows a strict rapport between the priestly oblation of Christ (cf. 5:25) and the sanctification of the Church (cf. 5:26), loved with a spousal love. Sacramentally inserted into this priesthood of exclusive love of Christ for His Church, His faithful spouse, the priest expresses this love with his obligation of celibacy, which also becomes a fruitful source of pastoral effectiveness. . .

Along with the firm conviction that Christ grants them this gift (of consecrated celibacy) for the good of the Church and for the service of others, the priest assumes it for his entire life. . . (n. 58)

Celibacy, then, is a gift of self "in" and "with" Christ to His Church and expresses the service of the priest to the Church "in" and "with" the Lord.

It should be pointed out that the *Directory* repeatedly emphasizes the freedom of the priest to respond to the call to the priesthood with its consecrated celibacy.

6. A Roman Catholic bishop always wears a ring. It is said that this ring symbolizes his wedding to the Church. In terms of his celibacy, the bishop can truly be said. to be "spiritually wedded to the Church," not in any divided way, but in total service to Christ and His people.

7. Speaking about the consecrated celibacy of religious, the document *Fraternal Life in Community* states:

In the community dimension, consecrated chastity, which also implies great purity of mind, heart, and body, expresses a great freedom for loving God and all that is his, with an undivided love and thus with a total availability for loving and serving all others, making present the love of Christ. This love, neither selfish nor exclusive, neither possessive nor enslaved to passion, but universal and disinterested, free and freeing, so necessary for mission, is cultivated and grows through fraternal life. Thus, those who live consecrated celibacy "recall that wonderful marriage made by God, which will be fully manifested in the future age, and in which the Church has Christ for her only Spouse" (n. 44).

8. Interestingly, he also told me his wife belonged to another church. I am sure this proved to be a tension also!

9. See Chapter 3, "Celibacy: A Sign of Love."

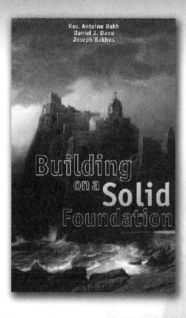

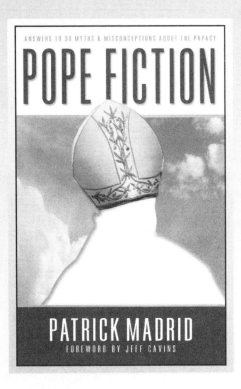

How to Order

BASILICA PRESS

W5180 Jefferson St.   Phone: 800-933-9398
Necedah, WI 54646   Fax: 608-565-2025
                     Email: cathsales@tds.net

PO #:_____   Date:_____

Bill To: Ship To:

Name:_____   Name:_____
Address:_____   Address:_____
City:_____State:____Zip:_____ City:_____State:____Zip:_____
Phone:_____
Email:_____

QTY	ISBN	Description	Unit Price	Total
	1-930314-07-8	Catholics In The Public Square $4.95		
	1-930314-06-X	A Will to Live $5.95		
	9-781-930314-11-5	Draw Near to Us, O Lord $5.95		
	9-781-930314-10-8	When God Asks for an Undivided Heart $12.99		
	0-9642610-8-1	Surprised By Truth $13.99		
	0-9642610-6-5	Making Senses out of Scripture $14.99		
	0-9642610-9-X	Any Friend of God's Is A Friend of Mine $9.95		
	1-930314-01-9	Lessons from the Lives of Saints $12.95		
	1-930314-00-0	Bible Basics $19.95		
	0-9642610-0-6	Pope Fiction $14.99		
	1-930314-04-3	Building on a Solid Foundation $14.95		
	0-9642610-2-2	Nuts & Bolts $11.99		
	0-930314-07-8	Scripture Studies - Galatians $14.95		
	0-9942610-3-0	Springtime of Evangelization $9.95		

Subtotal	
Shipping	
Total	

Notes:_____

_____

Call for Bookstore & Parish Discounts
Call for exact shipping